BRAIN POWER

IMPORTANT NOTICE

This publication is designed to provide accurate and authoritative information in regard to the subject matter covered, but it is sold with the understanding that the publisher is not engaged in rendering legal, accounting or other professional service. If legal advice or other expert assistance is required, the services of a competent professional person should be sought. The publisher does not guarantee or warrant that readers who use the information provided in this report will achieve results similar to those discussed.

This manual is intended as a reference volume only, not as a medical guide or a reference for self-treatment. You should always seek competent medical advice from a doctor if you suspect a problem. This book is intended as an educational device to keep you informed of the latest medical knowledge. It is not intended to serve as a substitute for changing the treatment advice of your doctor. You should never make medical changes without first consulting your doctor.

Additional copies of this book may be purchased directly from the publisher. To order, please enclose $39.95 plus $4. postage and handling. Send to:

Book Distribution Center
Post Office Box 15196
Montclair, CA 91763

Printed in the United States of America
0 9 8 7 6 5 4 3 2 1

Table of Contents

Introduction
Your Personal Wonder Machine

The most powerful, wonderful and complex computer on earth is the human brain.

We all have one.

We all enter this world fully equipped with our very own supercomputer. Throughout our life times, this wonderful biological machine will run our bodies, handle our emotions, enable us to think with cool logic and dream with wild abandon. Our brains are the vehicles we ride to experience higher spiritual states of awareness.

The brain stores our precious memories for us. Unlike a photo album or even a video library, our brains let us keep all aspects of our past experiences alive — sight, sound, smell, touch, taste — all for the asking whenever we want to re-experience them.

With just a tiny effort we recall the warm smell of baking bread, or remember vividly the sensation of hot sunshine touching our bare backs. Tucked away in the brain is the look of our children the day they were born. We can relive the sound of rushing waves on a beach with an effortless command.

Even the latest technology and the best science has not been able to produce a marvel of computing power that is the human brain. While the world's most advanced super-computer costs millions of dollars to produce, we are each given free a computer that is one thousand times superior to even the most powerful man-made machine.

Such is the marvel of the human brain.

But as you know, this miraculous biological computer inside our skulls is not foolproof or problem free. We are too painfully aware of what happens when things go wrong with the brain.

For the elderly, it is often the dreaded Alzheimer's Disease — a baffling condition that renders the brain "spongy" and causes people to lose their minds, including their ability to take care of themselves, or even know who they are.

For other people, a brain problem may be simply loss of memory — bad enough in itself to considerably reduce the quality of life of the individual whom suffers from this common kind of impairment.

Yet another mighty enemy of a healthy mind is depression — very often called America's No. 1 health disorder.

On any given day, some 71 million Americans are suffering from either mild, moderate or sever depression. For the worst, the only way out is suicide. For millions of others, it makes for lives of drab, daily misery.

But problems with the brain do not have to be crippling and debilitating diseases like Alzheimer's or Clinical Depression.

Some people just wish they had more power of concentration. Some people, especially children, lack proper attention spans. Some people are not so much depressed as they are sluggish and fatigued — lacking the energy to make their dream and goals come true.

Who would not like to increase their ability to think and solve problems faster? Who wouldn't want a memory so powerful not a single fact could slip from it's grip even scores of years later? Who wouldn't want to maintain a healthy, active mind well into old age so that not a single joy of life would have to be turned away or denied?

That's what this book is going to be all about. It's about the brain, the worlds most complex and advanced super-computer, and how to keep it running is tip-top condition.

We're going to look at some of the latest treatments for those agonizing life robbers, such as Alzheimer's and Depression.

We're going to look into the latest technology in memory enhancement, improvement, even memory repair, including the recovery of lost memories.

We're going to lay out to you in clear and concise details, all the incredibly easy and effortless ways you can make your brain think more clearly, more powerfully and with greater skill and precision.

In short, we're going to show you how to get smarter fast!

Sometimes, performing this miracle can be as simple as changing your diet. That's right! The scientific research is conclusive that certain foods are truly "brain foods." That is, they make your brain function more cleanly and efficiently, leaving you more clear-headed, smarter, faster and happier.

By the same token, many other foods and drinks have been identified as true "dumb foods," foods that literally make your more stupid. A hint: a lot of them contain alcohol, refined sugars and greasy fats. By eliminating these from your diet, you Brain can function more smoothly and with fewer inhibitions.

Another quick and painless way to supercharge your mental power are with something called "smart drinks." These are actually healthy concoctions of various fruit juices, vitamins, minerals, herbs and something called "neurotransmitters" which boost your mental powers amazingly — and all you have to do is sip them down. They taste great and they make you feel even greater!

Modern medical science is also working vigorously to invent new prescription drugs that can treat diseases of the brain and mind. If you thought Alzheimer's was a condition without hope, and a disease that could only lead to further despair and loss of mind, have hope! There are now a number of drugs that are not only stopping Alzheimer's dead in it's tracks, but actually reversing the process of mental decline for some patients.

There's still no fool-proof cure for brain diseases like Alzheimer's, but there are solid answers and treatments for thousands of people who are suffering needlessly. Don't you owe it to someone you love to look into the possible treatments that could give them back the very thing that makes them who they are — their mind and brain?

Finally, there is an enormous amount of accumulated knowledge about how to improve the brain and make the mind more sharp and healthy without looking to foods, food supplements like vitamins, or drugs.

Did you know there was a way to "tune up" your brain using patterns of sounds and lights? This is one of the most exciting areas of cognitive enhancement research.

Today, there are many "off the shelf mind machines" which you can purchase right now for the purpose of improving the functioning of your brain. Thousands of people swear by their positive effect on their brains.

And there are new ways to actually exercise the brain as if it were a muscle. Just as lifting weights can increase the size and strength of a biceps, certain "brain exercises" can make people smarter, develop better memories, become more creative and all around more clear headed and happy.

Brain exercises work by increasing blood flow to the brain, bringing more oxygen to the brain and by encouraging the neural connections in the brain to become more complex, and thus more able to handle higher levels of mental functioning.

You may have heard the often repeated statement: "Most people use only 5 percent of the brain's capacity." Well, scientists tell us tat statement is true, and some of those same scientists are now saying there are ways to get the rest of that 95 percent off the bench and into the ball game! We're going to update you on the very latest in this exciting area of brain research and personal performance enhancement.

Amazingly, some of the best brain tonics are not those uncovered by cutting edge medical science and nutrition research. Indeed, we can look equally well to ancient, sometimes even forgotten, tradition and knowledge to make the brain and mind all it can be.

Ancient techniques of meditation, massage, acupuncture, acupressure and thousands-years-olds herbs treatments — such as those that come from the magnificently aged Ginkgo tree — can help tune the brain to peak performance as well or better than some of the most advanced technology.

In this book, we have looked everywhere — from the near future to the mists of the distant past — to uncover every conceivable weapon against dysfunction of the brain. But we didn't stop with brain problems. We also wanted to find ways to make a healthy brain and mind even better. If you're already smart, you can be even smarter. If you're memory is okay, there are ways that you can make your memory a powerhouse of information storage.

Brain Power is designed to give you peak mental power for the rest of your life, no matter how old you get and how long you live. It is our hope and goal that the time and brain power you expend reading this book will translate into true power for the supercomputer given to you by Mother Nature — your brain.

Chapter 1
The Brain and Food

Read this chapter carefully. In it we are going to reveal to you:

- Common foods that can make you more intelligent
- Common foods which prevent depression
- Which foods to avoid to keep your mind clear
- Which foods keep you thinking straight
- Which foods to avoid to keep away depression
- Which foods to avoid to prevent mood swings
- Which foods can stop hyperactivity in children
- And more...

But first, a true story ...

Tommy K. was a problem child. At age 11, he was already a full-fledged terror. His favorite things to do were hit, kick and destroy. Place a new toy in front of him, and Tommy would smash it. Leave him alone with his playmates, and it wouldn't be long before a fight broke out —

and Tommy was always the instigator. No day care center would agree to take Tommy on a client. No baby sitter would agree to stay with him for a single evening, or one afternoon.

Tommy's parents were at wits end. They were good, decent people with good jobs, and were well liked and respected in their neighborhood. They were kind, loving parents.

But with Tommy, they had tried everything. Sessions with psychologists, behavior modification programs, time-outs, punishment-reward systems, even prayer — but through it all Tommy remained a hyperactive, willful, even violent child, destined for a future of social isolation, juvenile detention or worse.

What was really painful was the fact that Tommy's parents had already raised two perfect children. They had proved to themselves and the world that they were good parents. Their 14-year-old son, Justin, and 12-year-old daughter, Emily, were model students, happy and delightful children. Yet, here was Tommy, the baby of the family, who seemed intent upon a life of violent destructive behavior.

But then Tommy's mother, Margery, happened upon a magazine article about nutrition and its effects on the human brain and mind. She learned that certain foods could effect mood and that some foods could have an extreme effect on the behavior of people, and that children were especially vulnerable. Further, she read that some children who were deficient in the common vitamin B1, and other vitamins, could display noted antisocial behaviors, and other psychological problems.

Margery showed the article to her husband, Ben, and suggested Tommy's problem was lack of Vitamin B1 or some other vitamin in Tommy's diet. Ben was skeptical, but at this point, he and his wife had tried everything, so he was ready to look at any alternative. So while Marge and Ben didn't dare hope that a simple vitamin deficiency could be behind their child's monstrous behavior, they had nothing to lose.

They took Tommy to their doctor and he ordered a blood test, and also a saliva test to look for deficiencies of all kinds. The doctor also ordered a CBP, a Complete Blood Profile. A week later, Margery and Ben had their answer.

The tests showed that Tommy was remarkably deficient in not only vitamin B1, but in the full range of the B vitamin family. Although uncertain about the cause, the doctor speculated that Tommy lacked some kind of enzyme that allowed his body to assimilate B vitamins. So even though Tommy ate a well balanced diet rich in B vitamins, his body was unable to process it. The doctor ordered a regimen of B-Complex injections, and later, oral supplements of B-Complex vitamins.

The results were miraculous. Tommy changed — no, it would be more accurate to say that Tommy transformed. The brooding, violent little demon had become a happy, well-adjusted kid, full of sunshine smiles, bursting energy and a tremendous capacity for love. It almost seemed as if Tommy wanted to love more now to catch up for all the years he lost in darkness.

The difference was that his brain was betting the integral nutrient it needed to allow Tommy to be what a human being is supposed to be — loving, constructive and positive, looking to the future and asking: "how can I contribute to make the world a better place."

Not bad for a few little B-Vitamins!

The Brain and Nutrition

Just a few years ago, medical doctors could never have believed that a person's behavior could be affected by what they ate, or did not eat. For most of medical science history, researchers have believed that it did not matter what a person ate when it came to the nutritional requirements of the brain.

Scientists long ago concluded that the brain uses only one nutrient to keep itself running: glucose. And no matter what a person eats — be it junk food, such as candy and soft drinks, or healthy foods like fish and vegetables — only glucose finds its way to the brain after the foods have been digested and broken down into their more fundamental elements in the stomach and digestive system.

The brain is protected by what medical doctors call "the blood-brain barrier." This is a series of partitions made up of various kinds of bodily tissues that keep the brain separate from the rest of the body.

Scientists have always believed that the brain was protected from any kind of fluctuation in the nutritional intake of an individual by the blood-brain barrier. Since only glucose arrives at the brain for processing, what that glucose comes from is immaterial. Just about all foods contain glucose, even foods that are considered unhealthy. So even while an obese person is damaging his heart with a high-fat diet, his brain is oblivious to the problem from a nutritional standpoint.

But now scientists know that there is a direct relationship between what we eat — or don't eat — and the healthy functioning of the brain. Many foods, for example, affect the mood. Some foods when you eat them can actually make you feel depressed, angry and negative. Others can do just the opposite — they can make you feel lighter, happy and positive. Indeed, research scientists have been stunned in recent years to discover that what you eat can even give you a poor memory — or a stronger one. Ask any good teacher today if a the diets of their students make them fast learners or slow learners, they will tell you that a child suffering from poor nutrition is all but unteachable!

What's more, several studies have showed children who are sent off to school with a sugar-filled breakfast in their stomachs do not perform as well or learn as well as children who eat a well balanced breakfast containing high vitamin foods, like fruits, high fiber foods like whole cereals and foods containing complex carbohydrates and small amounts of protean.

To put it more plainly, a child with a stomach full of milk and sugar is likely to fall asleep at his desk while a child full of fruit, cereal and a dash of milk is awake, alert and ready to learn.

So it's clear today that what you eat makes a huge difference in how your brain functions. What you eat can not only make you depressed, but in some cases, people with chronically poor diets have been drives to gross antisocial behavior — everything from committing crimes of violence and property damage to turning their bad behavior on themselves, including the ultimate act of despair, suicide.

And all because they were simply feeding their brains the wrong diet! They were eating the wrong foods!

It's not only eating the wrong things which can produce negative emotional behaviors and feelings.Not getting enough of the right nutrients can produce the same unwanted conditions.

Deficiencies in a number of vitamins and minerals can do damage to the way the brain functions, as well as the entire nervous system by which the brain regulates and controls the rest of the body. The absence of just one vital nutrient can cause trouble for the brain, and the content of just one meal can mean the difference between a good day and a terrible day in the mind of the individual who had eaten it.

In fact, some mental conditions that were once considered untreatable and hopeless can be completely cured by an adjustment in food intake!

So now, as promised, let's take a look at a brain healthy, "feel good diet.

Happy Fat

Fat always gets a bad rap. Everyone is trying to avoid fat in their diets these days. Fat is a heart killer. Fat can make you overweight, unattractive, hypersensitive, and so forth.

But now we know that getting too little fat can wreck you mood and make you feel blue.

Recently a group of scientists looked at moods of 20 people, ages 20-37, before and after they ate a diet of 41 percent fat per day, or 25 percent fat per day.

One month later, the people who were getting less fat reported being much more depressed, feeling blue and even angry more often who ate the higher fat. The people eating the higher fat foods were routinely more happy, less depressed and had a greater general sense of well being. The researcher concluded that fat stimulates a hormones which can influence the brain chemical serotonin, which is at the center of this whole subject of mood. People with low serotonin have long been known to suffer depression, greater anger and other negative behaviors.

Thus, the solution seems to be too not severely limit your intake of fat if you also have trouble with your mood. Also, you can eat "good" fats and avoid "bad" fats. Good fats are primarily monounsaturated fats, such as that found in olive oil and fish, and not fats found in red meat.

It's Good And It Makes You Happy!

This sounds almost too good to be true, but scientists say that chocolate — yes chocolate — is an excellent mood lifter.

In new studies, scientists read sad stories and played sad music to a group of volunteers who became depressed. They were then given their choice of chocolate, milk chocolate or carob, a chocolate-like substitute made from palm

---

oil. It was later determined that those who ate chocolate were able to bounce back to happiness easily, those who ate carob did not. Milk chocolate helped, but not as mich as chocolate. Furthermore, the more depressed the people were, the more they craved chocolate.

The scientists concluded from this that chocolate contains serotonin-boosting substances, along with fat, which we already have said was a mood enhancer. Chocolate may also contain other chemicals that boost mood, although they have not been identified yet.

Fish Is Truly Brain Food!

Perhaps when you were little your mother or grandfather told you: "Eat your fish! It's brain food!" Well, guess what? They were probably right! Scientists now believe that people who do not like to eat fish probably have a much greater chance of getting depressed. When looking at world populations, researchers have noticed that measured rates of depression drop among populations that eat a lot of fish.

People in Japan more fish than any other people in the world. And guess what? The Japanese have the lowest rates of depression in the world. Scientists think a fat in fish called omega-3 boosts the kind of brain chemistry that makes people feel light and happy. Also, researchers in the U.S. have determined that doses of omega-3 fatty acids in pill form can help ease manic depression in people who suffer from this dread mental disease. In fact, in some cases, eating omega-3 capsules, or simply eating one meal of fish per day, helped a group of test subjects beat depression and recover from a variety of mental problems relating to depression and other mood disorders.

Vitamin D

We have long known that vitamin D — which you get from sunlight and milk — prevents the bone disease rickets. But scientists know think it fights depression as well.

Many people get depressed in the winter when sunlight is less, and people are forces to stay indoors longer and out of the sun due to cold weather. This may be robbing people of vitamin D, and thus, may cause depression. Researchers in England administered either 400 IU (International Units) or 800 IU vitamin D or a placebo (a fake pill) to a group of 84 people for a period of 14 days in late winter. Those receiving the pills did not know what they were taking.

The results were that those getting the vitamin D pill reported a sudden lift in mood. The people getting the fake pill reported no change in their late winter blues.

Why does this work? One answer may be that Vitamin D like, chocolate and fish, boosts levels of serotonin in the brain. Serotonin is the brain chemical linked to good mood.

But before you go out and load up on vitamin D, be warned that too much D is known to be toxic, so take no more than 200 IU per day if you are from 19 to 50 years old, 400 IU if you are between 51 and 70, and 600 IU for the over 70 folks. Good sources of vitamin D exists in salmon, fortified cereal, and we said, milk.

Beautiful B

As you read in the story of Tommy K, vitamin B is a powerful brain substance. Perhaps the "B" in this case should stand for brain. If you have too little vitamin B, you may get depressed, or worse.

In one recent study of 357 people over a 7 year period, those taking a high daily dose, in this case, 10 times the recommended daily dose, of nine vitamins for a year reported feeling a lot better about life from day to day, and that they had "far less" incidents of depression. The B vitamins, especially, (B1), riboflavin (B2) and B6 were cited as being the most effective in improving mood.

If you eat more of these food, you will get more natural vitamin B in your diet: dried beans, whole grains, fish, dairy products, poultry, eggs, bananas, and avocados.

You can also take a daily supplement of vitamin B in pill or capsule form, and any brand you find in any drug store is generally sufficient to get the job done. It's probably not a good idea to take 10 times the daily requirement of vitamin B, but doubling your dose should do you no harm.

Don't expect to get an "instant boost" or expect that popping a vitamin B will pull you out of a deep depression in an hour or two. Your moods will improve over time, so be patient and think happy thoughts with the help of vitamin B!

Conclusions ...

So there we have a good start to feeding the brain for optimum feel good effect. But we're only just getting started. In coming chapters, we are are going to introduce you to a number of items that you can provide for your brain to make it work better — some of these include herbs, hormones, more vitamins, exercises for the brain and a number of other special brain boosting techniques and treatments.

We'll continue our fascinating discussion in the next chapter.

NOTES:

_____

_____

_____

_____

_____

_____

_____

_____

_____

_____

_____

_____

_____

Chapter 2
Trust in the Power of Your Brain

L earning to trust in the power of your brain is the first and foremost step to unleashing the unlimited potential of your mind. This may sound too easy-after all, we believe we're making relatively good use of our brain, don't' we?

The truth is we are barely scratching the surface. Scientists estimate we are using only about 4% of our brain. That means we have a lot of room for improvement!

Probably the greatest barrier that keeps us from accessing more of our brain power is the fact we simply do not believe the power exists. We are able to live our everyday lives just fine-getting up in the morning, driving to work, spending time with our families, running our households. Who would think we need-or have-even more power available to us inside our heads?

If you want to improve the power of your mind, the first step is simply believing that your brain holds ample opportunity to do so. Simply trust that your biology has given you a brain with unlimited potential.

This chapter will take you through twelve steps designed to help you build your brain power. You will learn what types of thoughts, attitudes, and behaviors inhibit or enhance your brain's capacity to work in your favor and improve your life. You'll be given exercises to help you create new ways of using your mind and increase your brain power. Lastly, you'll be given ideas for creating an environment around you that stimulates your brain's growth.

Step 1: Understanding the Power of Attitude

The old saying is true, "You are what you think." Other than trusting that your brain is innately powerful, the second most important thing to building your brain power is the having the right attitude.

What is the "right attitude"? Does it mean following a rigid set of rules about who to be and how to behave. No, it most certainly doesn't. It means developing thoughts about yourself and your life that are healthy and conducive to increasing your brain's potential.

So often our attitude about ourselves and our situations are negative. And, unfortunately for us, we often carry around these negative attitudes with us year after year. We become "programmed"-we believe things about ourselves that aren't true. For instance, we may have told ourselves we are about as smart as we are ever going to get. Some maybe even refer to themselves as "stupid" quite often.

The thing about our brain is that it is more like a computer than your mother. It doesn't try to make you feel better when you throw negative comments at it; it doesn't try to convince you otherwise. It simply takes in information- negative or positive-and acts upon it. If you tell yourself you are never going to get any smarter, your brain will believe you and help make sure you don't. On the other hand, if you tell yourself you are smart and that your brain has unlimited potential, your brain will believe that just as strongly. So you can see how important it is to have the right attitude if you are going to increase the power of your brain.

Ask yourself these five questions to test your current attitude about your intelligence:

1. How would you describe your intelligence at various stages throughout your life; as a young child, as a teenager, as a young adult, as an older adult?

2. What attitude do you have about the power of your brain right now?

3. Did anyone ever tell you that you were not smart? When?

4. Did you believe that person?

5. As you look back, do you see how this comment affected your attitude about your intelligence and the power of your brain?

How you think about yourself-your attitude-deeply affects your ability to increase your brain power and live a more full life. That's why next to trusting that your brain is very powerful, establishing the right attitude is extremely important to boosting the power of your mind.

It may take some time to establish the right attitude . After all, it's taken a long time to establish the wrong attitude. First, you have to uncover and identify all the attitudes that hold you back from reaching your potential. This can be tricky because your attitudes "feel" like you-they are such a part of who you are that you may not be able to see them right away. With a little practice, however, and a desire to really make it happen, you can change your attitude.

Step 2: Using Motivation to Shape Your Attitude

One of the most powerful tools for changing your attitude is motivation. Motivation is not about getting "psyched up" for something. It's about establishing your choices and always moving forward in the direction that leads to your goal. For example, if you choose to become a great swimmer, your motivation automatically kicks in. You're excited about your goal, and you do the things that will help you become a great swimmer: sign up for swimming classes, go swimming and practice as often as you can, take the swimming tests that allow you to advance to the next level. It's easy because it's something you want to do. There's no "psyching up" necessary.

That's what true motivation is all about.

In the case of building the power of your brain, your motivation comes from choosing to trust that your brain is infinitely powerful, and making it your goal to tap into more of that power.

So many people go about it backwards-they think that they need to motivate themselves in order to reach the goal. Quite opposite is true. Rather than working on your motivation, work on making up your mind and setting your goal. Then, the motivation will take care of itself.

Some days it might seem harder to reach your goal-your motivation might as a result feel low those days. To help you confirm your choices and increase your motivation, you might try using affirmations.

Affirmations are simply a way to reprogram your brain into a new way of thinking about something-often a much healthier way for you and one which can help get you to your goal. An affirmation "affirms" that you can and will do something. Although you can substitute words that better fit your conversation style, your affirmation should send you a positive message about who you are and/or what you want to accomplish, as in this affirmation below:

"I am an intelligent human being. My brain is very powerful. I will build the power of my brain."

Say it to yourself when you get up in the morning, at midday, and at night before you go to bed. Say it out loud-using your voice in a clear, confident way actually increases the affirmations affect on your mind. Repeat it three times each time you say it. Use affirmations to help boost your confidence at any time you find yourself doubting your abilities.

Don't be afraid to use affirmations. If you're not used to telling yourself good things about yourself, or if you're not used to setting goals for what you want to accomplish in your life, they might feel silly at first. But persevere. Study after study confirm the power of affirmations to help change people's attitudes for the better. It takes time for your mind to assimilate the new ideal you've told it to set for yourself. And don't' be afraid to make up other affirmations that reinforce the changes you want to make in your life.

Step 3: De-programming Your Mind to Improve Your Attitude

Our attitudes about ourselves and our abilities shape our potential to tap into the power of our brains. We can start changing our attitude by making choices about who we are and what we want, and by using tools like affirmations to help set up a new ideal in our minds.

But there are a lot of old teachings in our head that can get in the way of this process. Do any of these comments sound familiar to you?

* I am stupid.
* I'm too lazy to learn. I'm not motivated enough.
* My teacher made me feel dumb in class.
* I've never been allowed to work in my own way.
* I was teased for being too smart.
* I was put down whenever I shared my ideas.
* I was creative once, but I'm not anymore.
* I can't change now.
* I don't deserve it.

Most people have some level of negative programming that they were exposed to as children. Unfortunately, children are impressionable and believe what they are told. As children grow into adulthood, they continue to carry with them these old messages about their seeming inadequacies. These ideas simply aren't true, but they feel true to the individual because they have allowed their mind to accept them as truth. Their mistaken beliefs about themselves keeps their mind imprisoned from unleashing its natural powers and keeps them from living more fulfilling, happier lives.

Ridding yourself of negative programming doesn't happen overnight. It takes a conscious effort on your part to identify false beliefs about yourself and to work on creating new ones that truly reflect who you are and want to be.

So often your negative programming is deep below the conscious level-you might not even realize just how much your behavior is shaped by these limiting beliefs. Your job is to overcome the doubt and mistrust you have in yourself. Your job is to regain what is naturally yours-a powerful mind-by leaving behind the old negative programming and learning to believe that you are a smart, highly capable human being.

A term used for the process your mind uses to program itself-whether intentional or unintentional on your part-is neurolinguistic programming. This simply means that the neurons, or brain cells, in your brain respond to language, or linguistics. Your brain is listening intently to the words you use and judgments you make about yourself and your situation. If you refer to yourself as a poor speller, your mind will hear your words and believe you. It will help insure that you are, indeed, a poor speller-until at such time you choose to change your thought about your spelling ability.

It is precisely because we can change our thoughts that we can change our entire attitude about who we are and what we can accomplish. Our brain is just as receptive to positive thoughts about ourselves as negative ones. We simply need to believe differently about who we are and what we want to accomplish. In the case of building our brain power, we need to believe that we are smart, and that we can learn to tap into our mind's unlimited abilities.

Once again, affirmations are a powerful way to help reprogram your mind to accept healthier beliefs about yourself. Tell yourself you have a powerful brain. If you can believe the negative messages you've listened to throughout your life, you can just as strongly believe the positive ones you are now telling yourself. Be patient as you practice affirmations. Your old beliefs have a powerful hold on you. You have several years of living your life based on these negative beliefs-it will take you awhile to undo the old thinking and create a new, more positive attitude.

Step 4: Combating Negative Thinking

Research studies show that children receive up to five times as many negative or critical messages each day as compared to positive messages. It's no wonder so many of us have become conditioned into believing we are not smart, not worthy, no good-the list goes on. In reality, nothing could be further from the truth.

As mentioned earlier, we often don't even realize just how powerful a hold these negative thoughts have on us. After years and years of believing that this is who we are, the messages live quietly deep down at a subconscious level. They feel like "me". And exposing them can be quite a challenge. As challenging as it may be to uncover all those old negative messages, it will prove to be one of the most liberating and wonderful things you can do for yourself. You will then be free to really experience the true power of your mind and begin to do things you never thought you could do.

There's really no magic to exposing the negative thoughts that keep you believing you are less than you really are. Actually, the best defense against old negative programming is a strong offense. You can literally change what you believe about yourself by simply telling yourself differently. It's that easy-in principle. What you will come up against, however, is those stuck old beliefs that will tell you "uh-uh," that your new, positive messages about yourself could never be true. They will try to discourage you every chance they get.

Remember, those old beliefs are comfortable right where they are, and any attempt to dislodge them will result in a fight that might make you feel like just giving in. Don't do it. It took a long time for those old negative beliefs to become deeply rooted. It'll take some time to dig them loose and plant a whole new set of positive beliefs about yourself instead.

If you're feeling like a "fake"-a trick your old belief system will use on you- you can calm your doubts by telling them you are "pretending" - you can increase your brain power. It's a bit less threatening to pretend, but what eventually happens is that you will start to believe it. And, then, it will happen!

Step 5: A Framework for Brain Function

It's important to understand the stronghold your old beliefs have on who you are today. Once you have an awareness of how they got there and that they are no more you than the man on the moon, you can confidently move forward to create a whole new set of beliefs about who you really are and want to be.

This new framework about negative and positive beliefs and how they shape your potential is the foundation to building the power of your brain. You must first believe that it is possible to develop your brain power. Then, after that, you must continually remind yourself-or affirm-this exact thought several times a day. Over a period of time, your body will adjust to this new belief about yourself, and you will have increased brain power.

A mental model of your brain's capabilities and how it functions will also help support your new belief that your brain is infinitely powerful. Many times we think of the brain as a lump of gray matter that sits inside our heads. It is that, it's true, but our brains are so much more. And by breaking it down into its separate functions, we can begin to get an appreciation for the complexity-and potential power-that resides unassumingly between our ears.

Think of your brain as an athlete. The best athletes understand the components that make up an excellent performance-whether on the track, an ice arena, or gymnasium floor. And they understand that these components must not only be strong in and of themselves, but must work at optimum when coordinated together.

In athletic terms, then, think of your brain as having four major components that affect its ability to perform its best:
1) strength
2) flexibility
3) endurance
4) coordination.

Let's start with strength.

Strength: Athletes lift weights and do other exercises that promotes the strengthening of their muscles. They do this in order to improve their overall ability to hold a handstand, for instance, or throw a shot put. With focus and intent on becoming stronger, they continue to lift weights or exercise and their muscle strength builds over time.

This same principle of is true for your mind. Your current mental strength can be measured by your ability to take on a challenge, like doing a math calculation or attempting to solve an important issue. If it seems hard to work with the problem, your mental "muscle" might be weak. On the other hand, if you tackle most problems quite easily, you probably have good, strong mental muscles.

Flexibility: In addition to being strong, athletes also need some degree of flexibility in order to perform at their best. Gymnasts, for instance, need a very high degree of physical flexibility. Hockey players, on the other hand, don't need as much flexibility within their body to perform well at their sport.

Your mind also has within it a degree of flexibility. How quickly you can go from one task to another demonstrates the flexibility of your mind.

For instance, the telephone rings when you're in the middle of preparing your taxes. It's your friend who wants to describe for you his plans for building a garage. Your ability to switch from number crunching to conceptualizing a blueprint demonstrates your mental flexibility. Your mental flexibility is also evident whenever to take an issue and can look at it from all sides-not just one.

Endurance: It's quite obvious from watching any kind of sporting event that athletes need to have endurance. Whether it's a soccer game or weekend figure skating competition, athletes need the stamina to remain strong, focused, and inspired throughout the entire event in order to perform well.

How does athletic endurance translate to your brain? There are many times when strong mental endurance gets us through writing a term paper in school or sitting through a day-long workshop. Our own performance-either what we produce or what we get from participating in an event-depends on our ability to remain sharp and focused throughout. We need to be able to shake off fatigue and boredom in order to perform at our best as well.

Coordination: There isn't a serious athlete alive that doesn't understand the need to be succinctly coordinated. You can't successfully flip from from the high bar to the low bar in mid-air during a gymnastics competition if you aren't coordinated. A gymnast needs to know where her body is in relation to each of the bars, the floor, and to itself-is her head or are her feet pointed toward the ceiling at any one time?

The same falls true for your mind. Mental coordination means being able to know what's going on around you and having the ability to orientate yourself to your situation.

For instance, maybe you in the middle of a very important report for your boss, have left work to go see your daughter play soccer, and will be taking your son and five of his friends to cub scouts later that evening.

Your ability to remain focused on what you are currently experiencing-in this case, to be excited about your daughter's participation and about the team's performance during the game-and yet manage in the background your other responsibilities of the report and son's cub scout meeting-is an example of good mental coordination. Your mind is aware of where you are in relation to the responsibilities around your life. And it can successfully manage them all.

Step 6: Exercising Brain Muscle-Sharpening Attention

One of the most effective ways to build your brain "muscle" is to enlist the power of attention. Great athletes pay attention both in training for a competition and actually performing in one. Without focusing their attention during practice and conditioning, they won't be prepared for a great performance. And we've all seen examples of the kind of razor-sharp focus during their athletic performance that makes the difference between a silver or gold medal.

If you want your brain to increase its strength and flexibility, you need to become good at focusing your attention. And there are some simple excises you can use to help you build the ability of your mind to pay close attention at all times.

One attention-focusing exercise you can do do is what we call "Every Second Counts."

Every Second Counts
1. Find a clock that has a second hand. If you can't find one nearby, you can use a watch with a second hand on it.
2. Seat yourself comfortably in front of the clock, or place the watch where you can see it without straining.
3. Breathe deeply three to five times. Relax you mind.
4. Now focus your attention on the second hand of the clock or watch. For two full minutes, keep your attention focused on the second hand. If you find your attention wandering, gently bring your focus back on the second hand and start over for two minutes more. Repeat this process until you have focused your attention on the second hand undisturbed for two full minutes.
5. Practice steps 1-4 each day until it is easy for you to keep your attention focused on the second hand for two complete minutes undisturbed. Then increase the time you are focusing to five minutes; then seven minutes; then ten minutes. Practice this exercise at least once per day for a minimum of a month. Remember, the more you practice the stronger your brain will become!

Another brain-enhancing exercise is simply paying attention to how well you are paying attention. That means you "observe yourself" in as many situations as you can-the more often you pay attention to how well you pay attention, the sharper your mind will become. Here's one scenario of how you might observe your ability to pay attention:

Observing Attention

Pick up a magazine or photo album with photos and captions in it. Notice how well you are able to focus in on each photo on the page-do some pictures attract you more than other? Do you seem to skip by some quickly with little interest in them? What gets your attention and what doesn't? Do you catch yourself thinking about other things like work or projects around the house rather than concentrating on the photo you are looking at?

Whenever you feel your mind wandering, pull it back in and concentrate on the photos or illustrations at hand.

Use this exercise to sharpen your attention by learning to focus fully on what you intend to look at or study.

Step 7: Exercising Brain Muscle-Smart Student Syndrome

Not all students have high IQ's, it's true, but being "smart" has as much to do with attitude as with your score on an intelligence test.

As you learned in the beginning of this chapter, you are what you believe you are. If you believe you are smart, you will be smart. It's all in your attitude. Everyone can remember someone in school who wasn't particularly genius, but was considered "smart." Why? Probably because they thought that they were.

Start believing right now that you are a smart student. Hard to think of yourself as student? Don't think of it in the classroom sense-we are all students of life, learning each day no matter how old we are. So, become a smart student right now and "catch" the attitude smart students have about themselves. Although you might not be in a classroom anymore, you can still apply these principles to everyday life.

10 Attitudes of the Smart Student Syndrome

- You are as capable of teaching yourself as any "teacher" you might have standing on behind a podium in front of you.

- Just listening and completing assignments dictated by a teacher is not enough. Know that the whole point of being a student is not to simply repeat back what you've been told or have read, but to assimilate and dissect information in learning to think for yourself.

- All the subjects of study are not equally important in your life. Rank and prioritize them according to your needs and interests.

- In prioritizing subjects, however, don't disregard the ones you are less interested in. Continue to study and ponder them. Staying engaged in studies that don't automatically excite you is actually a great way to stretch your brain's abilities and power.

- Understand grades for what they are and don't get too hung up on them. They are subjective measurements often controlled by the whim of one instructor or reflect an obscure curve of averages.

- Know that making mistakes is a sign of improvement-it means you've gone beyond your comfort zone into an exploration of something new. Feel good about laughing at your mistakes and proud that you are an adventurer.

- Also know that focused study can at first seem tiresome and frustrating. It's through perseverance that you will gain not only knowledge you didn't have before, but confidence in your ability to tackle and accomplish something that seems almost overwhelming at the beginning.

- Trust that it's your attitude and dedication to study rather than your IQ that means the difference between being a successful student or not.

- Learn and strive in your quest for excellence to please yourself-not your teachers or peers. The praise of others rides the surface of your emotions and is short-lived. Building your own self-esteem and sense of accomplishment runs deep within your character and will last you a lifetime.

- Find playfulness alongside the seriousness of study. Know that learning is a life-long process, and although vitally important, is meant to be an enjoyable, fun part of the game of life.

Step 8: Exercising Brain Muscle-Smart Studying

In addition to "catching" Smart Student Syndrome-adopting the attitudes that can help you come to believe that you are indeed smart-you can practice some simple study habits that will help you study more effectively and with less frustration as well as work to sharpen your mental strength.

Smart Studying: 10 Brain-Building Tips

- Know your purpose for studying the material you're about to read. What will you be gaining? How will it benefit you?

- Recall anything you already know about this subject. It can establish a framework for you and help you make connections as you embark on your study.

- Look at the bigger picture of your subject by distilling out the main points and understanding how the subject fits into a greater whole. In other words, don't get lost in detail. Discover the major themes and the effect these themes have on related things in life.

- Anticipate the next point the author is going to make. When the material follows a logical sequence, this can be fun, and it is certainly a way to help sharpen your mind and increase what you remember.

- Look for and identify the most prevalent questions and topics within this field of study. Learn the particular jargon the field uses. What are the premises from which this field of study operates? Understanding how the field is organized will be of tremendous help in learning about it.

- Pay attention to how your own mind reacts to the information you are studying. Do you agree or disagree? Are you in mild or strong disagreement? Why might that be; why do you feel the way you do? Does the information raise even more questions for you; is there more you want to learn about? Note your reactions. Following up on them will broaden your base of knowledge.

- Remember that not all the information available to you on a given subject is essential to read-besides, you'd never have time to study everything there is. Learn to evaluate and rank what's available so that you can focus in on what's really going to give you your bang for your studying buck.

- Create your own outline of an author's material as you go. Paraphrase and summarize. Even create symbols or pictures that represent the material you're learning about. Translating subject matter into your own personal mental model-complete with pictures-is actually a powerful way to build your brain's ability to remember well.

- Give your mental model a flip switch. In other words, find a word, story, picture, rhyme, or other phrase that succinctly captures your mental model of the material in a way that, when you simply say or think about it-you flip it on-brings it to memory complete and whole.

- Relate the material you're studying to what you already know. Making connections between old knowledge and new knowledge will help firmly root the new information in your brain. It simply takes its place naturally within your base of knowledge and becomes effortless to remember.

Step 9: Understanding Your Personal Intelligence Strengths

For years intelligence has been measured by IQ tests. According to recent insights about how our brain functions, scientists now know that IQ tests measure only two out of seven regions of intelligence in our brain-IQ tests are not reliable measures of intelligence!

The work of psychologist Howard Gardner has helped redefine the kinds of thinking our brain is capable of-and thus the fact that just because we are not as strong in one or two areas doesn't mean we aren't genius in a few others!

The Seven Areas of Intelligence

Gardner's theory describes seven areas of the brain that are responsible for how capable we are of interacting with the world in different ways. Understanding these seven areas of intelligence and evaluating our own mental strengths and weakness against this can help us realize just how smart we really are, and help identify areas where we can improve. **Here are the seven areas of intelligence that Gardner identified:**

1.**Logical-Mathematical:** the ability to understand sequential and/or numerical relationships.

2. **Linguistic:** the ability to use language well and communicate concepts clearly.

3. Bodily-Kinesthetic: the ability to use and control the body.

4. Spatial: the ability to think in images and organize them within space and time.

5. Musical: the ability to hear rhythms and musical scales for performing and creating music.

6. Interpersonal: the ability to communicate with others and interact with them.

7. Intrapersonal: the ability to communicate effectively with yourself.

You may have heard of "left brain / right brain" theory. It also states we have multiple intelligence, and that these areas of intelligence lie either on the left or right sides of the brain.

For instance, our creativity, like music or art, is said to be a "right brain activity". Mathematics and other logical thinking is said to be a "left brain activity." Even more proof that this is so is in the case of brain injury. An injury on the left side of the brain impairs logical thinking and language; an injury on the right impairs artistic ability.

What does this mean for you and your ability to build your brain power? It means that you can let go of old thinking and believe that you have an intelligent brain! You don't need to be a great mathematician to be considered "intelligent" or "smart" anymore-you simply need to find the areas of intelligence which you are are good at and develop your natural talents even further. Remember than your ability in one area of intelligence is just as legitimate as the mathematician's skill in another-you maybe can't do numbers like a genius, but then again, the mathematician may not be able to build things like you can if you are a "genius" in spatial relationships. With a new understanding of how your brain thinks, you can hone in on your intelligence strength.

The evaluation that follows will help you identify your intelligence strengths. Just check the phrases that apply to you-these phrases should describe how you are. At the end of the evaluation check and see which categories have the most check marks in them. These categories will be the ones in which you are most intellectually strong.

Logical-Mathematical Intelligence:

___ Were you favorite subjects in school math and the sciences?

___ Do you like puzzles, games, and other brainteasers that challenge your logic?

___ Do you like information that is numerically represented, like measurements, percentages, or quantities rather than information that is theoretical and without much fact or data?

___ Is it easy for you to figure calculations in your head?

___ Do you like to experiment with known data and changing that data around to discover what happens?

___ Do you find yourself evaluating the data and facts people are giving you for inconsistencies?

___ Are you always looking for logical relationships, rhythms, or patterns in the events and activities you participate in?

___ Do you keep up with the latest technologies and scientific discoveries?

___ Do you believe that there is a rational and logical explanation for everything?

___ Is your thinking void of imagery or words; does it come to you in abstractions?

Linguistic Intelligence (Words/Language)

___ Were you favorite subjects in school English, history, or social studies?

___ Are your favorite jokes plays on words, puns, or humorous misuse of the language?

___ Are books your primary way of gaining information?

___ Do audio media like radio or audio cassettes interest you more than visual media like television or movies?

___ Is it easy for you to formulate your words in your mind before speaking; is finding the right words when writing fairly effortless?

___ When speaking with others, do you refer often to things you've recently read?

___ Are you often consulted for the meaning of words or the organization of grammar?

___ Are you good at word games like Scrabble?

___ Do you pay more attention to billboard signs than the scenery when driving?

Bodily-Kinesthetic Intelligence:

___ Are you active/have you always been active in sports and athletic activity?

___ Are you outside as much as possible?

___ Are you well-coordinated?

___ Is it hard for you to sit still for long periods of time?

___ Do your best ideas come when you're involved in an athletic activity: walking, running, kayaking, etc.?

___ Do you prefer working with and creating things with your hands: pottery, carpentry, weaving, etc?

___ Do you touch things often in order to learn more about them?

___ Do you learn a new skill better by doing it rather than reading about it or watching a video about it?

Spatial Intelligence (Images/Pictures):

___ Were you favorite subjects in school art or geometry?

___ Do you prefer visual puzzles like crosswords, mazes, and connect the dots?

___ Are you drawn to magazines or books with lots of pictures, colors, and other images like diagrams or charts?

___ Do you prefer a camera, video recorder, or sketch book for recording an event rather than note taking?

___ Do you tend to sketch or draw often?

___ Can you visualize all sides of an object if looking at it from different angles-upside down, from the left, from the right, etc.?

___ Do you take particular note of colors and visual patterns wherever you are?

___ Do you see pictures or images when you close your eyes?

___ Are your dreams vivid and alive with lots of images?

___ Do you navigate well in an unfamiliar area despite not having a map?

Musical Intelligence:

___ Do you have a pleasing singing voice?

___ Do you play a musical instrument or have the strong desire to do so?

___ Do you find yourself tapping out rhythms while working or studying?

___ Do musical selections play over and over in your mind; do you sing or whistle to yourself often?

___ Is it easy for you to remember the words and music to all types of musical selections?

___ Do you spend more time listening to music than reading or watching television/videos?

___ Can you reproduce a piece of music you've heard only once?

___ Would you feel devastated if all forms of music were denied to you?

Interpersonal Intelligence (People):

___ Do you prefer team activities and sports over activities or sports you do alone?

___ Do you prefer entertainment and social activities that include groups of people, like playing cards or games, over solitary forms of entertainment like reading a book?

___ Do members of your family or people at work come to you for advice and guidance?

___ Do you seek the advice and guidance of friends and family when you have a problem rather than wrestle with it alone?

___ Does your circle of friends include at least five you could call close?

___ Are you comfortable within a crowd, whether the people are familiar to you or not?

___ Do you enjoy teaching others what you know?

___ Do you find yourself a regular part of community-based activities?

___ Do others consider you a leader; do you consider yourself a leader?

Intrapersonal Intelligence (Self):
___ Are you meditative; do you often spend time alone in contemplation and inner reflection?
___ Are you driven to learn more about yourself?
___ Are you often evaluating your progress toward the goals you've set for your life?
___ Do you have a hobby or interest that you keep private?
___ Do you or have you attended workshops that promote personal growth?
___ Do you have opinions not necessarily shared by the public around you?
___ Are you an independent thinker with a strong self-will?
___ Using your study of yourself and the feedback you get from others, do feel you understand your strengths and weaknesses?
___ Do you keep a journal for recording your reflections and evaluating your personal growth?
___ Do you prefer getaways that are rustic and private rather than bustling with people?
___ Are you self-employed or do you have a strong desire to be?

By understanding your personal intelligence strengths, you can come to believe that you are smart because you see how intelligence is not measured only by one's ability to calculate numbers. There are several kinds of intelligence, all important to creating balance within the melting pot of humanity. Your "smarts" are just as important as anyone else's!

Secondly, knowing where you are intellectually gives you a kind of "map" that can guide your efforts to enhance your brain . Once you have identified your personal intelligence strengths, you can hone in on them to excel even further your abilities in those areas. Plus, you can choose to develop your weaker areas since you now know what they are.

Step 10: Personal Intelligence Exercises

After assessing your personal intelligence strengths and weaknesses, you can begin moving in the direction that builds your brain in all seven areas.

Here are some exercises for each of the seven areas of intelligence that can get you well on your way to higher intelligence:

1. Logic/Numbers (Logical/Mathematical Intelligence):
* Number Crunchers
The following questions are meant to make you think exponentially and stretch your numerical and logical muscles!

1. How many words have you said in your life to this point?

2. How many doors are there in all the houses and other buildings in your hometown?

3. How many quarters would you have to stack to reach the top of the Empire State Building?

2. Words/Language (Linguistic Intelligence)
* What's that Word?

Whenever you're reading something, note any words that are unfamiliar to you and jot them down. Make it a point to find time before the end of the day to look up their meaning.

* Memorization

Choose a speech, poem, essay, or other short piece of writing that you particularly like and memorize it. You might try memorizing one to three lines a day until you have it completely memorized. Recite the piece out loud as you are memorizing it; keep the memory fresh by saying it out loud even after you've memorized the whole piece.

* Vocabulary Builder

Choose two to three words out of the dictionary each day that are unfamiliar to you . Start at the beginning of the alphabet and work your way to the end. Uses these words in sentences and notice if you run across them in anything else you are reading.

* Reviewing the Classics

Read books written by the great writers: Ernest Hemming, Thomas Melville, Virginia Woolf and Henry James for example. Notice the grammar. Look for clever and powerful uses of words and sentence structure. Try and note what makes for each individual's style.

* Book Report

Read a book and do a report on it. Describe the theme, plot, characterization, setting, and other details about the story. Compare it if you can to books that are similar to it: why is it as good or not as good as others? Also, say whether you personally liked the book and why.

* Audio Attention

Listen to books and other works by writers and poets on audio cassette tape. Again, pay attention to grammar, word usage, and sentence structure that makes for powerful writing. And since it is audio, listen to the way the story is being read; Does the reader's intonation add to the effect of the story? Is the reader using dialect for effect?

3. Physical/Body (Bodily-Kinesthetic Intelligence):
* Picking Grains

Choose a grain-like barley, rice, millet, or any grain easy for you to obtain-and transfer 100 grains from one bowl or plate into another bowl or plate with a tweezers. Your goal is to do this exercise as quickly as you can without spilling any.

* Physical Practices

Learn to do karate, tai chi, judo, akido, yoga, or any type of dance. Along with physically strengthening the body, these practices instill discipline at the same time.

4. Images/Pictures (Spatial Intelligence):
* Art Attraction

Visit an art gallery and choose a painting that really attracts you. Try to figure out why you like it so much: what's the artist's strategy behind the design and composition? Commit the picture to memory with as much detail as you can. Recall the picture later and look at each little detail in your mind's eye.

* Memorization

Choose a map, diagram, blueprint, chart, or any kind of illustration representing something in the real world. Study the illustration and analyze it for its accuracy and success in representing the real thing in detail. Try to picture the thing as three-dimensional.

* Any-And-All Perspective

Choose any object within your range of vision and try to "see" it from any angle: underneath, left and right sides, crossways, from the top. Notice the detail from each view. Then physically walk over to the object and look at it from all the angles you just imagined. How close was your image to the real thing?

* Movie Masters

Watch the film making of great movie makers like Alfred Hitchcock, Oliver Stone, and Steven Spielberg. Aside from highly technical special effects, what else do these directors use to compose powerful shots: colors, camera angles, movement within the setting, etc.?

* Mind Draw

Draw from your mind's eye the inside of your dryer, a floor plan for a new addition to your house, the inside of your cupboards including the contents, or your entire neighborhood.

* Brain Teasers

Do jigsaw puzzles, mazes and other brain teasers. Start a hobby or follow an interest you have that includes working with images : photography, video, drawing, or architecture, etc.

* Imaging

Deliberately make it a point to practice imaging on your own. Close your eyes and imagine something from your past, like the faces of friends and family from your youth.

Imagine each in as much detail as you can. Choose any image you like, and imagine it in as much detail as possible.

5. Musical Intelligence
* Instrumental Study
Study a musical instrument that you enjoy. Learn about how it makes the sounds it does. Discover its versatility: in what kinds of musical compositions can it be used? Consider taking lessons and learning to play this instrument.

* Music Recall
Sit comfortably and relax as you call to mind soothing sounds from your memory: a favored song or movie theme, a church bell, chimes, a pipe organ, a sweet singing voice, the instruments in an orchestra, the wind whistling at the window, the rain pattering on the roof.

* The Daily "Grind"
There are sounds within everything you do or find yourself in each day: traffic, washing clothes, passing by construction sites, etc. Become aware of the sounds in everything around you: do they contain a strange harmony, a shrill or sharpness, a drone, a regular rhythm, a grinding sound, etc.?

* Memorization
Choose to expand your musical experience by exposing yourself to different types of music on a regular basis.

* Compose it Yourself
Get creative! Make up your own tunes! Whistle, sing, hum, or do whatever you do best!

6. People/Others (Interpersonal Intelligence):
* People Watching
Go to a busy public place, like an airport or mall, and simply sit and watch people. If it helps, pretend you are an alien being on earth for the first time. What kinds of things are people doing? What can you learn about them by their behavior?

* Silent / Foreign Film Watching
Turn the sound off or watch a movie in a language you are unfamiliar with. Simply by watching the facial expressions and body gestures of the actors, try to understand the basis of their conversations and what's happening in the story.

* The Listener
Turn off your own judgments, emotions, and opinions and listen to someone else for at least ten minutes a day. Study what they say, how they say it, their facial expressions, and their use of other body language like gestures or posture.

7. Self/Inner (Intrapersonal Intelligence):
* Historical Models
Read biographies and autobiographies of people in history you admire. What was it about them that made them stand out in their time? What were their ideas like? What did they conclude about themselves and their lives in relations to their society and times?

* Self Collage
Create a collage that represents you. Include pictures and images cut out of magazines, drawn by you, or gathered from other sources, i.e., the outdoors. Glue all the

images that represent who you are onto a piece of tag board. What can you conclude about who you are?

* Personal Eulogy

Write your own eulogy as if you had died. What would you say about yourself, the type of person you were, your goals and ability to achieve them? What did life mean to you? What messages do you have for your loved ones?

* Dream Log

Write down all your dreams for a week. Include as much detail as you can. Think about the ones that were most vivid for you. Practice being each character and understanding what role each plays in your life. Ask them why they have appeared in your dream and what they have to say. Establish a practice of logging your dreams and interpreting them in this way.

Step 11: A Simple Understanding of Brain Physiology

A Baby's Brain

The brain's growth in a young fetus is amazing. The nervous system begins forming within 20 days of conception. The brain begins to develop around the 35th day. A fetus' brain cells, called neuroblasts, are generated at a rate of several thousand per minute. By 12 weeks, brain cells are multiplying at a rate of 2,000 per second, assuming the mother is supplying the fetus with the proper nutrition. A malnourished fetus can lead to as much as a 50 percent loss in brain cells compared to the average. At 20 weeks, the entire nervous system is developed with 15 billion brain cells in place, compromising only 2 percent of body weight but requiring 20 percent of the body's oxygen supply.

Babies have an estimated 100 billion nerve cells, or neurons, available to them when they are born. Neurons are concentrated in what most people know as "gray matter", which is actually the layer on the outer surface of the brain's cortex. The brain processes about three billion stimuli every second to remain in a waking state.

As was stated at the beginning of this book, scientists estimate we use only about 4% of our total brain power. It's obvious we have lots of room for improving our own ability to think!

The Old Age Brain

It's true that as we age, our brain cells die. We lose about 50,000 neurons a day, or around 18,250,000 per year. By the time we are 75 years old, our brains weigh about 10 percent less than they did when we were born.

Although it may seem this news is not good news, it actually isn't bad. In fact, there need not be a drop in the power of your brain at all. It's not necessarily the number of neurons you have that make you smart. Neuroscientists conclude that the human brain is flexible and resilient, adapting for dying neurons by growing more and stronger connections between the remaining ones. These connections are what allow the brain to process complex problems. The important thing is to keep the networks between the neurons-the networking branches are known as dendrites and the junction points are called synapses. As you learn more and stimulate your brain, you grow more dendrites and synapses.

By practicing mental exercises like the ones throughout this chapter, you can keep the connections between the neurons strong and help insure a strong mind through to the end of your lifespan.

Step 12: Strengthening the Brain Network

Here are some mental exercises you can use to strengthen and build the dendrites and synapses between your brain cells.

* Numbers Games

Practice working with numbers. For instance, count backwards by a number not usually used in counting quantities, i.e., 3, 4, or 7. Second, keep doubling a number for as long as you can, i.e., 4, 8, 16, 32, . . . For an even more vigorous brain work-out, try visualizing one of the following scenarios as you practice one of the above numbers exercises:

1. Watching the world series

2. A day at the fair

3. Building a brick gate around your house

* Anchoring

1. Sit comfortably in a chair. Close your eyes. Take a few deep breaths to help you relax and establish an easy breathing pattern. Feel your mind and body relaxing.

2. Think of a time in your life that you felt totally accepted, happy, successful, and joyful. It might have been something you experienced in a relation-

ship, or came about as a result of a new break-through or insight you had.

3. Go into this memory and fully experience it again. Try to picture and feel all the details around you. Feel the sensations in your body. Describe every-thing-what you see, hear, sense, and feel-using present tense as if it was happening right now.

4. When you feel you are fully present in the experience and feeling all the sensations of pleasure and happiness, touch your earlobe or wrist for at least five seconds. Imagine yourself anchoring this very wonderful memory that, when you touch it again, evokes the same feelings in you immediately

5. Wait at least ten minutes, then touch the area that you anchored your pleasant memory to. Do you experience the same wonderful feelings? You can touch your anchor point anytime you want to trigger a positive state of mind. This is called a positive conditioned response, and works to combat your negative conditioned responses talked about earlier in this chapter.

6. You can even link your anchors to help bring on more than one state of mind. For instance, let's say you have a big test. You might want to first call up an anchor that evokes feelings of calmness to ease your anxiety. Then you might want to call on another anchor that brings forth a feeling of confidence. Finally, you might stimulate an anchor that elicits a simple feeling of gratitude and recognizes your great ability to think and learn.

Step 13: Reframing Past Memories

Every memory you have has a certain emotional quality to it. It is easy to recall the pleasant memories that make us smile and feel happy. It isn't so easy, however, to recall old memories that were painful or heartbreaking.

It's those old, painful memories that can give us a lot of trouble in our lives. They are the ones that make us believe we aren't adequate in some way, i.e., a teacher telling you you're stupid or a parent sending the message that what you do is never good enough.

This negative programming takes a strong hold in our belief system and attitudes the more emotion we attach to it.

How can we diffuse painful, negative memories? We can learn to reframe the memory and how we feel about unpleasant experiences in our past. You can change the emotional intensity of the memory by going back to it and remembering it differently-through a new lens. It's a lens that lets you adjust the picture in any way you choose to literally change how you feel about that experience.

With age and experience behind you, you may be able to see an old memory in a new light. Your brain unconsciously assigned emotions to your experience that linger on in your memory of it. Now you have the power to change that adjusting the lens.

Use the following eight steps to adjust the lens in which you view your memories, good and bad. Practice first with good memories. Notice how your new adjustments change how you feel about it. Then try it with unpleasant memories. Again, notice how adjusting your lens changes the memory and your emotions toward it.

Adjusting the Lens
1. Clarity-You can choose to blur or sharpen the image.
2. Distance-You can choose how far away you are from the scene.
3. Duration-You can choose to quickly scan an image or focus in for a good look.
4. Movement-You can choose to stop the action for a close examination of an image. Or, you may choose to fast-forward through certain parts of the memory.
4. Scope-You can choose to only see the foreground, or get an expanded view including details of the background as well.
5. Contrast-You can choose how much light, dark, and gray are in this memory.
6. Transparency-You can choose to give the image a transparent quality which lets you see through it to what's behind.
7. Color-You can assign bright, vivid colors or dull, quiet colors to any parts of the memory you choose.
8. Image Orientation-You can choose to move the image around in a way that lets you look at it from different angles, i.e., the top, the bottom, left, right.

Step 14: Creating a Brain-Healthy Environment

There are factors in the space around you that can affect your brain's effectiveness. Below are some ideas for creating a brain boosting environment:

- Negative Ions: Negative ions (negatively charged air molecules) have been scientifically measured to improve mood, increase concentration, and inspire creativity. Waterfalls are one of the earth's largest generators of negative ions-is it any wonder people feel refreshed after being near a waterfall?

- A View of Nature: You can also boost your brain power by being in a setting that gives you a view of nature. A study that measured alpha brain waves-the ones that elicit relaxation and creativity-found these waves increased when their subjects viewed a natural setting versus city scenery. If getting a room with a natural view isn't possible, try hanging up a picture of a nature scene.

- Full-Spectrum Lighting: Our bodies rely on natural light to trigger the release of brain chemicals that keep our mind alert. A lack of natural light can lead to problems like the need for more sleep and food as well as increase the risk of depression. Install full-spectrum lighting in your work environment to maximize your brain's full potential.

- Brain-Friendly House: Minimize the use of chemicals in your home, and make sure you have adequate ventilation throughout your house, i.e., fans, windows that open. Stay away from synthetic materials, i.e., carpets, shower curtains, paints, solvents, etc. Buy clothing and other household fabrics that contain natural fibers like cotton and wool.

Chapter 3
Special Brain Nutrition for More Brain Power

Just like our bodies, the brain has its own nutritional needs which affect how effectively it functions. For instance, there are some very specific chemicals scientists have identified that create states of mind like sharp mental alertness to relaxed states of drowsiness.

Plus, air is an important nutrient for the brain—about 20 percent of the air you breathe everyday is used by the brain to complete its tasks. You can learn just what food, herbs, and supplements affect the power of your brain. Then, you can use them to enhance your own brain power.

This chapter will introduce you to the kinds of nutrition your brain wants and needs for optimum performance. Although difficult to get years ago, you can easily find these items today in grocery stores, nutrition store, and specialty mail order catalogs.

Protein—A Basic Brain Building Block

We've all heard how important it is to get protein in our diet. Protein happens to be one of the most important building blocks for your brain. They contain important amino acids that are essential to proper brain functioning. It's well known that chess players eat a meal full of protein before a chess match. They understand the relationship between a high-protein meal and mental sharpness.

It's important to eat protein-rich foods like fish and other seafoods, poultry, beans, and red meat before eating the carbohydrates that are a part of your meal. Meats and beans contain an amino acid known as tyrosine. Tyrosine makes two types of neurotransmitters: dopamine and nor-epinephrine. Both of these chemicals regulate sharp thinking, long-term memory, and mental alertness. When tyrosine reaches your brain first, it will kick in to stimulate your brain and keep your mind clear and focused.

Carbohydrates, on the other hand, contain a protein known as tryptophan. This amino acid is used by the brain to create a neurotransmitter known as serotonin. Serotonin induces sleep and slows down nerve transmissions within the brain. If serotonin hits your brain first, you'll feel sluggish and your thinking will not be as clear. Some foods that contain tryptophan are milk and dairy products, grains, breads, and starchy foods.

If you want to be at your mental best, be sure to eat your meats and beans first. Save the potatoes and bread for last.

Sources of Brain-Building Protein

Mental alertness can be attained by eating high protein, low carbohydrate meals. If staying mentally sharp all day is important to your work, consider starting your day with a breakfast that contains high protein foods. Do the same for lunch—eat a good share of protein-rich foods and save the carbohydrates for last.

As evening rolls around, change things around. Eat a dinner of carbohydrates and let the relaxing qualities of serotonin help you wind down. You can see that by understanding the chemicals at play in your brain, you can regulate your diet to induce states of being from keen mental alertness to quiet, stress-relieving calmness.

There are several excellent sources of proteins that work to keep your brain at it's sharpest. And it's true what they say—fish is one of the best brain foods there is. Here's why: fish contains high amounts of tyrosine, which produces chemicals that stimulate the brain. It also contains a fatty acid known as omega-3 oil. This fatty acid is key to stopping disease processes that result from the overproduction of substances within the body. Omega-3 oils have also been successful at relieving migraine headaches.

These fish have the highest concentration of omega-3 oils: salmon, tuna, mackerel, bluefish, herring, sardines, lake trout , sable fish, and Atlantic sturgeon. These fish have more than 1 gram per 3.5 ounces of fish.

Shellfish are also an excellent source of nutrients for stimulating your mental performance. Shellfish are almost pure protein—they deliver brain-boosting tyrosine to your brain quickly and efficiently. The drawback to eating shell-fish is that they accumulate water pollutants in greater concentrations than finned fish. Yet, 3-4 ounces of shellfish as an appetizer or snack can give your brain a quick boost.

How Much Protein is Enough?

If protein is such good brain food, why eat anything else?

Well, the answer is simple. Your whole body requires a large variety of vitamins, minerals, amino acids, and other nutrients to keep it alive and healthy. Although a high protein diet is desirable for maximizing your brain's ability to function, you need to maintain a balance between protein-rich and other types of foods.

Your body weight, and how much your physically and/or mentally exert yourself in your lifestyle will help you determine how much protein to consume. For instance, and athlete whose daily routine includes expending a great amount of physical energy might tend to eat more carbohydrates, which break down easily in the body and can supply a constant source of energy. On the other hand, an individual whose daily routine includes consistent mental exertion may naturally find themselves drawn to foods containing more protein.

The trend in America in the past few decades has been to stray away from red, protein-rich meats in an attempt to reduce the also high levels of fat contained in it. Chicken and fish have become popular sources of protein, as have soybeans, legumes and other types of beans. If you need to be concerned about excess fat in your diet, yet want to include more protein-rich foods, try avoiding red meats and substituting chicken, fish, and beans.

Brain-Building Herbs

Protein isn't the only brain-boosting nutrient you can access to maximize the power of your mind. There are also several herbs that have been proven over thousands of years to be effective in helping the brain function at its best.

• Ginkgo Biloba

Ginkgo biloba has been used by the Chinese culture for for thousands of years as a way to increase oxygen flow to the brain, improve mental alertness, treat conditions like depression, dizziness, and ringing in the ears. It is also used to treat various people in various stages of memory loss and dementia.

Ginkgo biloba comes from a tree native to China and Asian countries—a species that is 300 million years old. It's leaves are said to increase blood circulation into the brain's micro capillaries. It's interesting that the leaves of the ginkgo tree resemble the anatomy of the brain's two hemispheres—its veins spread out in two directions which make it look as if there are two halves to it.

Ginkgo biloba is making it big in America these days. The herb can be bought over the counter at not only nutrition stores, but most any drug or dime store in the country, as well as through a variety of mail order companies. Below are the ways ginkgo is said to affect your brain:

- increases the circulation of blood and oxygen
- improves short term memory
- improves the transmission of electrical impulses through the nerves in the brain
- enhances metabolism within the brain, including the breakdown of glucose, a primary sugar used for energy
- keeps arteries with the brain flexible, preventing blood platelets from clogging arteries as well as preventing hardening of the arteries
- contains antioxidant properties that protect the brain and halts the damage done by free radicals to brain tissue
- slows down the aging process of the brain, which can improve mental functioning for the elderly
- enhances mental alertness and optimizes conditions for learning

Ginkgo biloba can be taken as a liquid and in pill form. For liquid form, take one that has at least 24 percent of the active ingredient. Dosage should be between 120 mg to 160 mg and should be spread out over three doses daily. That is because the herb stays in your system for between 3-6 hours. If taken in pill form, simply follow the directions on the package for the correct dosage and times to take the herb.

Ginkgo biloba generally tends to act slowly. Give the herb at least eight days before you look for its effects. It may be more than three weeks before you notice real improvements. Permanent effects take 3-6 months. There are no known side effects to ginkgo biloba taken at recommended dosages.

• Ginseng

Ginseng is another Chinese herb that is often revered as the "king" of herbal medicines because its qualities are said to be powerful for overall health and longevity. Ginseng has been used by the Chinese culture for over 4,000 years and is probably the most widely used herb in the Orient.

The ginseng root is the part of the plant used to for medicinal purposes. Since ancient times, ginseng has been referred to as the "root of eternal life." This might be in part due to the fact that the ginseng root resembles the human body. This form has led the culture to believe that the divine spirit lives within it. If this is so, it is no wonder the plant so effectively facilitates health-giving properties to the bodies it enters!

Ginseng contains a family of chemicals known as saponins, which increase the metabolism of certain brain chemicals and help keep your mind in top mental condition. It also works with your adrenal cortex to keep in balanced and decrease its tendency to zip you into an alarm stage when under stress. Keeping your adrenal cortex balanced helps you learn quicker and allows you quicker access to both short and long term memory. Thirdly, ginseng improves mental performance by increasing the level of norepinephrine in your system, a neurotransmitter that is vital to a positive mood and sharp memory.

Ginseng is an overall stimulator for health, and is said to affect the body in these positive ways:

- increases blood circulation to the brain and contributes to efficient mental processing

- balances blood sugar levels which keeps concentration, mental alertness, and memory sharp
- is an antioxidant ridding your body of free radicals
- reduces fatigue and helps resist stress
- boosts your energy while calming your body and mind
- balances the body's physiological systems in general; regulates heartbeat and blood pressure; improves digestion
- increases the efficiency of the endocrine glands and the rate of metabolism

Ginseng comes as a pill, extract, tincture, powder, paste, tea and dried root. As a liquid extract, 500-3000 mg are recommended spread out over three doses per day. People with high blood pressure should start at the low end and work up to higher dosages as their blood pressure stabilizes. Ginseng extract comes in two forms: a reddish color, which is stronger and appropriate for winter, and a whiter color, which is milder and more appropriate for use in the summer. For other forms of ginseng, follow the directions on the packaging. As with most herbs, the effects of ginseng are cumulative. Don't expect overnight results. With consistent use of ginseng, you can look forward to long-term effects over time. Although ginkgo biloba and ginseng are two of the most popular herbs for overall brain health, there are other herbs as well known for facilitating healthy brain function:

- **Ma Hung**

Ma Hung is also known as ephedra sinica. This herb comes from the stems of the joint fir tree. Ephedra is the botanical model for ephedrine, developed by pharmacists and used as a stimulant in cold decongestants and amphet-amines.This herb provides a boost to your energy stimulates the brain. It is often taken as a tea, one to two cups each day. This herb should not be used by pregnant or lactating women, people with high blood pressure, those with heart or thyroid conditions, and those with diseases like diabetes, glaucoma, or psychosis.

• Epimedium sagittatum

Epimedium helps improve memory and absent-mindedness by stimulating blood circulation in the smallest capillaries in the brain. It is also known as "horny goat weed."

Ayurvedic Mind-Building Practices

Ayurvedic medicine, the practice of health and well-being in India, is an ancient tradition predating even Chinese medicine, which is more than 5,000 year old. Ayurveda is both a science and philosophy that includes working with the body as a whole—considering the mind, body and spirit together—to promote healing and induce a state of optimum health.

Ayurvedic practitioners also consider the external environment, like the weather, foods, and other conditions under which a person lives as part of understanding illness and developing a therapy to restore the individual's health. Ayurvedic therapies are not quick-fixes. This tradition believes that the solution to a health problem needs to be slow-building and subtle. In that way, all levels of the individual experience the transformation needed to effect a permanent health change, which keeps the disease from reoccurring.

Herbs

• Gotu-Kola

Although gotu-kola is used mostly as a way to heal skin
afflictions such as wounds, varicose veins, and other irritable conditions, it is also recognized as helping to increase
memory and intelligence. Ayurvedic practitioners also
believe that gotu-kola helps combat aging and senility. Like
the leaf of ginkgo biloba, the gotu-kola leaf resembles the
brain in that its veins branch out into two separate hemispheres. This herb is used by Ayurvedic doctors to calm
the mind and increase the flow of energy between the right
and left hemispheres of the brain. Gotu-kola also contains a
chemical substance known as triter penes that act as a natural tranquilizer to calm the body and mind. The herb gradually builds up in the system to enhance mental stamina by
improving the brain's nerve response as well as detoxifying
and boosting the energy level of cells. Gotu-kola is most
often taken as a tea at bedtime to promote a restful sleep
and an alert state upon waking.

• Calamus Root

Calamus root helps to open up the flow of nerve impulses. Ayurvedic practitioners have used it for centuries for
purifying and revitalizing the brain and nervous system. It
has been used to treat epileptic seizures and other types of
convulsions. It is said to calm the mind and bring clarity. It
is also said to strengthen the memory, stimulate clarity and
sharpen awareness. Ayurvedic practitioners recommend
powdered calamus root be taken in 1/4 to 1/2 teaspoon
doses, mixed with honey. It should be taken twice a day,
once in the morning and again in the evening.

- **Bhringaraj**

It may sound exotic, but actually this herb grows in the southwest part of America. The name means "ruler of the hair" after its property to promote hair growth. It is also used as a brain tonic to calm the mind. It can take the form of a hot or cold infusion, used as a medicated oil, or taken as a powder (250 mg-1 gm).

- **Licorice**

Licorice, in herbal form, is said by Ayurvedic practitioners to have a powerful effect on strengthening the memory.

- **Nutmeg**

Nutmeg is an herb most people have in their cupboards, and it can be a tonic for your brain. Ayurvedic practitioners recommend a pinch in milk at bedtime to help you relax and calm insomnia.

- **Sage**

More than just adding flavor to your dishes, sage is used by Ayurvedic practitioners to elicit calmness and ease emotional strain.

- **Basil**

Even basil, thought of as a culinary herb and regularly found in people's cupboards, is said to strengthen nerves, improve memory, and increase sensory awareness and clarity. Ayurvedic practitioners recommend a simple basil tea mixed with honey.

Minerals & Gemstones

• Gold

According to Ayurvedic medicine, the electronic energy of gold can improve awareness, intelligence, and memory. It is also said to strengthen the heart, increase stamina, and calm the nervous system.

To take advantage of the power of gold within your body (and not just without!), take something made from gold and boil it in two cups of water until half of the water has evaporated. Drink one teaspoon three times daily. The energy imprint of the gold is said to have passed into the water from boiling it .

• Beryl

Beryl is a gemstone that comes in hues of green, yellow, or blue. Ayurvedic
practitioners recommend wearing this gemstone set in silver as a necklace or ring, worn on the left hand, to promote intelligence.

• Ruby
The red ruby is also a gemstone recommended by Ayurvedic practitioners to be worn to increase mind power, set in silver or gold as a ring worn on the left hand.

• Other Mind-Enhancing Gemstones

Ayurveda also recommends wearing the following gemstones to promote strong brain function: emerald, jade, peridot, pearl, moonstone, yellow sapphire, and topaz.

Foods

• Ghee

Ghee is a milk product made from cow's milk. It is said to improve memory, stabilize the mind and help correct mental disturbances caused by energy imbalances.

• Oats

Oats in any form—oatmeal, flour, oat milk—helps nurture the nervous system as well as strengthen brain power.

• Asparagus

This vegetable is packed with more than just flavor—it is said to tone the nerves and the brain.

Traditional Chinese Medicine Tips for Building Brain Power

Traditional Chinese medicine has some ancient but powerful wisdom for creating health in our bodies and enhancing the power of our brain to work at its best.

Like Ayurvedic medicine, traditional Chinese medicine considers the whole person when diagnosing and treating illnesses. This practice is particularly focused on a person's energy and attributes states of health as to energy that is either in balance or out of balance in some way. It has mapped out a complete energy anatomy that not only identifies each organ, but the complete energy system that the organ represents. These energy systems interact within themselves and with each other to form our health. Two common terms used in traditional Chinese medicine, yin and yang, refer to too much or too little energy (yin=calming, descending energy; yang=energizing, upward rising energy).

A balance of the yin and yang energy is needed for optimum health.

Below are some foods used by practitioners of traditional Chinese medicine to balance energy that has gone too far in either the yin or yang direction:

- Mushrooms: Mushrooms have long been recognized for their positive effect on health. Although many types of mushrooms exist, the reishi mushroom in particular is said to calm the mind and spirit.

- Oyster shell: Oyster shell most often comes in a powered form, and is said to create balance by increasing yin (calming) energy in the heart as it lowers yang (energizing) energy.

- Fruits: Lemons, mandarin, and mulberries are known to calm the mind and nerves, treat insomnia, and improve overall memory and concentration.

- Whole grains: Whole grains like wheat, oats, and brown rice can help calm the mind.

- Herbs: Many beneficial herbs have already been mentioned. Others that are calming for the mind and nervous system are chamomile, catnip, valerian, dill, basil and scull cap. They can be used as tinctures or are popular as herbal teas.

- Silicon foods: Foods that facilitate calcium metabolism help strengthen the nerves and heart tissue. They are foods like celery, lettuce cucumber, oat straw and oat groat tea, and forms of barley.

- Seeds: Seeds said to calm the mind and soul are mandarin seeds, chia seeds and jujube seeds.

- Dairy products: Goat milk, clarified butter, and and hormone-free milk nurture heart energy.

An Herbal Brain-Boosting Recipe

There are several herbs which facilitate a healthy, powerful intellect when used alone or in combination with other herbs. You have just scratched the surface on the vast use of herbs to promote health and well-being, and may want to study more in-depth on how herbs can help you be your mental and physical best.

In the meantime, here's one power-punched herbal recipe to help you begin seeing the benefits of herbs in your diet:

Ingredients:

- gotu-kola—increase memory and intelligence; combat aging and senility
- peppermint—for improving blood circulation in the brain and calming the nervous system
- Siberian ginseng—powerful herb that strengthens overall brain and body functions
- kelp—protects heart and nerve tissue from stress and tension

- wood betony—a mild sedative which reduces stress
- skullcap—treats insomnia and eases tensions that affect learning

Combine equal amounts of these dried herbs and pre-pare a tea or take as capsules according to directions on their packing. This combination will improve your concentration and memory as well as increase your mental stamina.

Consider using these herbs in combination with the recipe above, or on their own:
- bee pollen
- myrtle wood
- alfalfa
- echinacea
- cayenne
- sarsaparilla root
- blue vervain

Brain Chemistry

You could spend literally years studying the brain and how it functions; scientists continue to try unravel the mystery. There is no need to be an expert to learn how to help your brain function at its best. Yet, there are a few basics you should know about brain anatomy to give you a general framework from which to understand what make your brain tick.

• Chemicals

Information is passed along in your brain by chemicals known as neurotransmitters. Neurotransmitters helps send an electrical signal from one neuron, or brain cell, to the next. Here are a few that you may have heard of, or that you will soon hear of if you continue to study how your brain functions:

- Norepinephrine: Norepinephrine works like adrenaline or amphetamines—it excites your brain. It appears to increase blood flow to the brain, and puts the brain into a high state of alertness. It also appears to trigger long-term memories, particularly those that are highly charged or invoke fear.
- Endorphins: Endorphins are the "feel good" neurotransmitter. They are natural pain-killers, reducing the intensity of pain and irritation. With the help of endorphins, you have a sense of well-being that often leaves you feeling inspired and motivated to use your creativity and work hard without much effort.
- Acetylcholine: This neurotransmitter helps transmit the electrical current between neurons. The efficient transfer of electrical impulses between neurons affects the brain's ability to respond quickly to new stimuli and other forms of information. Acetylcholine also seems to be crucial to good memory function. This chemical requires a constant supply of oxygen and glucose, which is broken down to create energy, since it is repeatedly being put together and taken apart in the brain as it does its work.
- Gamma-aminobutyric acid (GABA): With several trillion nerve connections in your brain, this neurotransmitter works to keep the nerve activity under control. It is called an inhibitory brain chemical because it inhibits the transmission of nerve signals and keeps things in check.

- Serotonin: Serotonin also inhibits nerve transmission and helps control nerve activity. It is believed this neurotransmitter has something to do with regulating sleep in accordance with the day/night cycle. This brain chemical also regulates pain and affects your overall mood. For instance, too much serotonin can produce depression. Prozac, the popular antidepressant drug, actually prevents the brain from absorbing too much serotonin.
- Dopamine: Dopamine affects physical movement. Not enough dopamine in your system can bring on Parkinson's disease, in which the body twitches and moves uncontrollably. Too much dopamine can lead to convulsions and even schizophrenia.

Other neurotransmitters you may run across are: purine nucleosides, peptides, taurine, and tyramine.

Depending on who you talk to in the scientific community, scientists have identified from between 50 to 100 neurotransmitters that act as the carriers of information between your brain cells. An ample supply of these chemicals as well as the efficient crossing of them between brain cells is vital to sharp mental performance.

Processing Information

The cells within your brain responsible for sending information are called neurons. Neurons are specialized nerve cells that facilitate the electrical charge that makes thinking possible. The neurotransmitters are the chemicals that help send an electrical charge from one neuron to the next.

Here's how it works: Neurons receive information through what's known as a dendrite, which resembles a tree with limbs branching out from it. They send information through an axon. A space exists between neurons known as a synapse. It is within the synapse—where an axon meets a dendrite— that information is passed over. As the electrical charge from an axon makes its way across the synapse to the host dendrite, it is transformed into a chemical, or a neurotransmitter.

The information being sent or received might be a thought, an impulse, or a call to action. Your cells have differing electrical charges running through them—they range from .0075 volts from the inside of a cell to the outside. The information is interpreted by the cells in your body. It is these electrical pulses that are literally being sent, received and interpreted each second that keep your mind functioning and your body healthy.

This process of electrical exchange happens at about 100 meters per second, which is about one million times slower than the speed at which electrical impulses speed through a computer chip. Yet, the human mind has much more flexibility than a computer. A computer becomes bottlenecked when too much information is running through it within the same circuitry. The brain, on the other hand, has countless pathways for information to flow.

In fact, it is this continuous flow through infinite pathways that allows our brain to function and create thoughts, feelings, and action. Processing these electrical and chemical messages is what's also responsible for the state of your body, like being alert or sleepy or feeling pain. It is also what regulates your moods, affects things like dreaming, memory, intelligence, and even mental illness. That's why it's important to involve your brain in activities that assist it in developing stronger connections and help it operate at its most optimum level.

Free Radicals—Modern Day Damage

Almost everyone today has heard the term "free radicals." Since they were first discovered by Dr. Denham Harman at the University of Nebraska in the late 1950s, much work has been done by scientists to understand the origins of this substance as well as how it interacts within the body.

Free radicals are both necessary for the body and yet, when an excess of them exists, can actually do considerable damage. Free radicals are essentially a natural by-product of metabolism. Digestion and other processes within your body that break down compounds and release energy also release free radicals. They are oxygen molecules that are incomplete and unstable—having an unpaired electron that is free and available for quickly bonding with other molecules. Your body wants a certain number of them—it is free radicals that seek out and defend against invader cells like bacteria, viruses, germs and other toxins within the body. The population of free radicals are kept in check by specific enzymes whose job it is to rid the body of excess free radical molecules.

Today, however, artificial free radicals are introduced into our bodies at a rate faster than our bodies can get rid of them. Microwaves, x-rays, and other forms of radiation along with smog, cigarette smoke, chemical food additives, hydrogenated vegetable oils, and fat substitutes are all common factors of modern living and are sources of artifi-cial free radicals.

Too many free radicals running loose within our bodies can cause molecular combinations that are not needed by the body. The result is a molecular compound that is unnat-ural, unhealthy and potentially damaging to tissues and organs. Unstable free radical compounds can also mutate the DNA at the cellular level. Your brain is particularly sus-ceptible to the damaging effects of too many free radicals.

Antioxidants—Cleaning Out Free Radicals for Age-Proofing Your Brain

Many scientists believe that age is determined greatly by the rate that our organs, tissues, and body systems degen-erate. Free radicals are culprits that can cause areas of our body to function improperly and breakdown sooner than they would if they were left alone and remained healthy.

First and foremost, the strategy for protecting your brain against free radicals is to eliminate as many of the sources of free radical contamination from your diet and environ-ment as possible. Along with removing their sources, you can combat free radicals by ingesting antioxidants, a natur-al substance that works inside your body to rid it of excess free radicals that do exist.

Foods you should avoid include fat substitutes labeled artificial or unsaturated. Avoid fried foods as well, since the high heat associated with these oils actually causes the release of even more free radicals than would be present at room temperature. Drink purified water to eliminate heavy metals and other contaminants often present in treated water. Avoid cigarette smoke and other environments where smoke, fumes, and strong odors exist.

Along with avoiding foods and other environmental sources of free radicals, include in your diet several sources of antioxidants:
- vitamin E
- vitamin C
- vitamins B1, B2, B3, B5, B6, B12
- beta carotene
- ginkgo biloba
- ginseng
- zinc
- selenium
- folic acid
- copper
- amino acids cysteine, methionine, and taurine
- coenzyme Q10

You can take these antioxidants singly or in combination. Read the instructions for correct dosage amounts when purchasing any antioxidant, vitamin, or other supplement.

Here's a small synopsis of three popular antioxidants:

- Coenzyme Q10: This substance naturally occurs in the body where it works as an antioxidant while generating energy in brain cells. As it carries out this activity, it also protects neurons from free radicals and the damage they can cause.

Coenzyme Q10 is made from two amino acids, L-tyrosine and L-methionine. Physical states of illness like colds and stress can lower levels of coenzyme 10, as can the level of hormones in your system and the use of prescription drugs. Coenzyme Q10 can be found naturally in polyunsaturated vegetable oils like soybeans and monounsaturated oils like olive oil. Other food sources include spinach, peanuts, sardines, beef, white tuna, and walnuts. If taking coenzyme Q10 as a supplement, 10-90 mg daily are recommended.

- Zinc: Zinc is needed for many brain functions, one of which is as an antioxidant. Zinc works with copper to combat free radicals. There is typically ample amounts of zinc in your brain to guard against high levels of lead. If taking a zinc supplement, take copper as well since too much zinc depletes your copper supply. The recommended dosage for zinc is 15-30 mg daily in combination with 1-2 mg copper each day.

- Selenium: Selenium also occurs naturally in your body, working with vitamin E to defend your body against free radicals. It also aids other antioxidant enzymes to keep free radicals in check. Selenium can be toxic if taken in doses over 2,400 mcg daily. A recommended dosage is 250-350 mcg each day.

Power-Packed Sprout Juice

Sprouts from wheat and barley grass contain high amounts of chlorophyll, a powerful detoxifying agent that goes after invading bacteria and other mutant cells. The health benefits of these sprouts are intensified when processed as a juice. It is easier for the body breakdown and make use of chlorophyll and other vitamins and minerals that come from these sprouts.

Microalgae as Brain Booster

Like sprouts, microalgae are also high in chlorophyll. They also have the added benefit of being high in protein—more protein than is found in meats and soybeans.

The leader of the microalgae pack is chlorella. This plant contains up to 76 percent chlorophyll as well as a number of nutrients essential for top brain functioning. Another popular microalgae with brain-boosting benefit is spirulina. Follow package directions when adding microalgae to your daily brain-building diet.

Using Vitamin C to Boost Your Brain Power

Vitamin C is a well-recognized antioxidant. It plays a major role as an antioxidant within your brain. In fact, your brain needs 15 times more vitamin C than the rest of your body. Vitamin C travels through your body and brain neutralizing free radicals thousands of times a second—that's why it's important to keep an ample supply of this vitamin in your body.

In addition to fighting free radicals on its own, vitamin C assists the amino acid glutathione in accessing fatty membranes of the brain cells that vitamin C itself cannot penetrate. It also assists another free radical-fighting agent, vitamin E, by boosting its supplies when low.

The body does not manufacture vitamin C. It must enter the body through the food and nutrients you eat daily. Your body literally "pumps" vitamin C to parts of your body that need it most. Vitamin C in your blood is concentrated by 10 times and supplied to the cerebrospinal fluid. This is because the central nervous system is the most susceptible to free radical damage since it contains the highest amounts of highly unsaturated fats. The brain then receive its vitamin C from the cerebrospinal fluid in concentrations of 10 times the amount.

Brain cells need—and receive—vitamin C in 100 times greater concentration that anywhere else in the body. Clearly, an abundant supply of vitamin C is vital to healthy brain function.

How much is enough vitamin C? Recommended dosages are from 1000-3000 mg daily, in 500 mg doses throughout the day. People over 65 should take between 3-9 gm daily. Smokers need to consider that each cigarette robs the body of 25 mg of vitamin C. Vitamin C should always be taken with lots of water for proper absorption.

Choline-An essential substance for strong memory

Essential to a strong memory is a neurotransmitter known as acetylcholine. This brain chemical is necessary for your brain to be able to store new information clearly. It acts as a deliverer of messages between neurons. It is made from choline and acetate.

The supply of acetylcholine decreases as people age. Biochemical changes in the brain diminish the production of acetylcholine. Without an adequate supply of this important neurotransmitter, people will begin to suffer cloudy thinking and memory loss.

Choline supplements can revitalize the production of acetylcholine and restore it to healthy levels. And taking choline supplements may not be just for the old. Younger people with memory deficiencies can be helped permanently by taking choline.

Boost your Memory with Choline and Lecithin

Lecithin is a substance that is found in all cells within your body. It is particularly concentrated in the brain, making up almost 30 percent of the brain's dry weight. Lecithin provide the myelin, or fatty sheaths surrounding nerve fibers, with the nutrition it needs to be healthy. It also plays a role in the production of acetylcholine.

Choline alone is beneficial for assisting in the production of adequate amounts of acetylcholine. When taken together with lecithin, you have a powerful combination for assuring that an ample supply of acetylcholine is always there for your brain to complete its function of memory quickly and completely.

Once more tip: Choline requires vitamin B5 to convert to acetylcholine. Add this vitamin to your choline-lecithin combination to insure the acetylcholine-production cycle.

Follow the recommended dosage amounts on the packaging for choline, lecithin, or vitamin B5 in any combination of these you choose to use. People who are diagnosed as manic depressive should not take choline.

Food Sources of Choline
- wheat germ: 1/2 cup = 2,820 mg
- peanuts: 1/2 cup = 1,113 mg
- eggs: 2 large = 800 mg
- whole wheat flour: 1/2 cup = 613 mg

- white rice: 1/2 cup = 586 mg
- trout: 3.5 ounces = 580 mg
- pecans: 1/2 cup = 333 mg

Vitamins and other Nutrients that Replenish and Protect the Brain

Your brain is a complex organ and requires innumerous chemicals, vitamins, minerals, and other substances to keep if functioning at its best. There are several other nutrients you can increase in your diet or include as a supplement that can help you in your goal of minimizing the damaging effects of free radicals and increasing your brain power.

Vitamin E—Neuron and Brain Tissue Protector

Vitamin E is the most powerful fat-soluble antioxidant yet discovered. It is often referred to as a tocopherol—a group of eight compounds that are considered essential antioxidants. Vitamin E protects the membranes of neurons and brain tissue from free radical damage. Although not typically considered a brain builder, vitamin E works with selenium to protect what currently exists in the brain, fighting off free radicals so that the brain stays healthy. Because vitamin E and selenium work together, it is prudent to make sure your body is also receiving ample supplies of selenium.

Natural food sources of vitamin E are wheat germ, nuts and cold-pressed, unrefined oils from nuts, seeds, and soybeans, plus dark leafy vegetables.

Follow the directions on the package when taking vitamin E supplements. You can find it as a mix containing other tocopherols. Because vitamin E is fat-soluble, it means that it will be absorbed by fat tissue. Fat tissue is capable of storing what it absorbs, so it is important that you do not ingest excess amounts of the vitamin E—high doses can damage the thyroid, adrenal and sex glands.

Vitamin A—Free Radical Warrior

Vitamin A is also a fat-soluble antioxidant that works to protect neurons against the damages of free radicals. It is produced in your body from beta carotine. Beta carotine is especially effective in combating a particular kind of free radical known as a singlet. The singlet is a product of the natural metabolism of the body, but can also be introduced into your system through exposure to ozone, cigarette smoke and other forms of air pollution and environmental toxins, plus direct exposure to sunlight. It has the ability to cross over from the blood into brain tissue with ease, and thus your brain is highly susceptible to damage by this culprit. Beta-carotene is the only substance that can neutralize the singlet.

Natural food sources of beta-carotene and vitamin A are orange-colored vegetables and fruits like carrots, sweet potatoes, pumpkin and apricots; dark green vegetables such as spinach and kale; plus fish oils and animal livers.

Scientists estimate that as many as 37 percent of Americans are deficient in vitamin A. When you take vitamin A or beta-carotene supplements, be sure to monitor your zinc intake as well (20-25 mg daily). Zinc is necessary for vitamin A to be released from the liver where it is stored. Take vitamin A supplements or foods within a meal that has fats for better absorption within the body. Keep your intake to within 300 mg daily. Too much vitamin A can be mildly toxic.

The B Vitamins—Builders of Vital Neurotransmitters & Brain Energy

- B1: Vitamin B1 is also referred to as thiamine. Deficiencies in this vitamin can lead to mental disorders like depression, confusion, anxiety, loss of memory, and unusual obsessions. Thiamine plays a major role in the conversion of glucose into energy within your nervous system, helping make sure you've got the energy you need to carry out proper brain functions. It is also a powerful antioxidant.

- B6: Vitamin B6 is used in the production of important neurotransmitters. A deficiency in this vitamin can lead to mental deterioration since the production of vital neurotransmitters diminishes without it. Vitamin B6 also works to reduce stress.

Vitamins B1 and B6 can be taken in conjunction with the other B vitamins as a single supplement containing the minimum daily required amount for each.

Phenylalanine—Boosting Mental Alertness

Phenylalanine is an amino acid used to produce neurotransmitters, particularly noradrenaline. Noradrenaline gives the brain a boost of energy, improves memory, retention, and concentration plus sharpens the senses.

Phenylalanine gets used up quickly when a person is in a situation that is stressful, dangerous, or highly exciting.

Because of its ability to heighten energy and the senses, it can be used to sharpen alertness and ward off depression.

Phenylalanine can be taken alone on an empty stomach in doses of 375 to 500 mg. You can also take a form of phenylalanine called DLPA of between 1,000 and 1,500 mg twice a day, once in the morning before breakfast and in the afternoon to induce a high state of mental clarity and energy.

For an energizing drink, add two teaspoons of bee pollen, two tablespoons of honey, 25 drops of ginkgo biloba and liquid ginseng, and a dropperful of DMAE to your powdered phenylalanine combined in a glass of warm water.

Glutamine—A Natural Source of Energy

Glutamine is an amino acid that works in the brain to produce a chemical known as glutamic acid. Glutamic acid is another brain-boosting energizer the sharpens your overall mental capacity to think and process information clearly and quickly.

Glutamic acid helps to neutralize ammonia in your brain. Ammonia is a natural by-product of protein metabolism in your brain. Too much ammonia can cause nausea and irritability. Other symptoms of low levels of glutamic acid, or high levels of ammonia, are fatigue, mood swings, confusion, and the inability to concentrate.

Because it actually creates energy, an ample supply of glutamine is more effective for creating alertness than coffee or other product containing caffeine, which simply stimulates the nervous system and then is gone.

Recommended dosage of glutamine supplements is 250-500 mg, building up to 1.5 gm daily.

Arginine—The Memory Builder

Arginine is an amino acid that seems to be very important to maintaining a strong memory and preventing the onslaught of aging on the brain. Arginine is an amino acid that is converted by your body into spermine, a chemical found in brain cells, blood tissue, and semen. Low levels of semine are often followed by memory loss and/or senility.

Arginine has been produced synthetically and studies have shown it to be very powerful in reversing the effects of aging. The cost of synthetic arginine is prohibitive for the general public, however, costing in excess of $20,000 per year for an effective prescription. As an alternative, nutritionists have created a formula containing three important brain nutrients that, when combined, make for a highly effective anti-aging, memory-enhancing combination that is affordable for the average consumer:
- arginine, 6g
- choline, 600 mg
- vitamin B5, 500 mg

Germanium—More Oxygen, Less Toxins for Your Brain

Geranium is actually a trace element found within the earth's crust—it is listed as an element on the periodic table of elements used by chemists and scientists. Germanium is also found in minuscule quantities in herbs like ginseng, garlic, and chlorella.

Scientists have recently discovered the benefits of geranium as a brain booster with its ability to stimulate body tissues to accept more life-generating oxygen; because of this, it is sometimes referred to as vitamin O. It also acts as a detoxifying agent, capturing dangerous heavy metals like mercury within your body and ridding it within 24 hours. Tests have also shown that germanium boosts the immune system and has a positive effect in combating cancer, tumors and viruses in doses of 100-300 mg.

What this translates into as far as a benefit to your brain is that you will have enough oxygen for your brain to carry out mental demands as well as clean out any heavy metal toxins that could impede your brain's ability to function.

Natural food sources of germanium are garlic, ginseng, aloe vera, pearl barley, watercress, comfrey, plus shitake and reishi mushrooms. Supplemental organic germanium sequioxide should be taken according to directions on the packaging, usually 30 mg for preventative maintenance, 50-100 mg for minor problems, and 1-1.5 gm for pain relief.

Oxywater— Delivering Oxygen and Detoxifying the Brain

Besides germanium, there is yet another way to deliver more oxygen to your brain—by drinking small quantities of diluted food-grade hydrogen peroxide (H_2O_2). It's called hyperoxygenation, or oxyv̄ater for short.

Oxywater works like germanium in its ability to rid the body of toxins and contaminants. It also delivers generous amounts of oxygen to the brain and body. Research has shown that regular use of oxywater improves intelligence, alertness, memory and reflexes. It has even shown to have some positive effects on both Parkinson's and Alzheimer's diseases.

Oxywater comes in premixed commercial formulas that can be found in nutrition and health food stores. You can also make your own by adding 2-10 drops of food-grade hydrogen peroxide to about six ounces of pure spring water. Drink this mixture at least three times daily.

Oxywater does give off hydroxyl radicals as it metabolizes hydrogen peroxide. You may want to take antioxidant nutrients like vitamins, A, C and E or herbs like ginkgo biloba in order to neutralize excess free radicals.

Boosting Brainpower and Helping Kids be Smarter

Evidence continues to mount in the medical community as to the powerful effects of nutrients on children. Children who are deficient in certain types of nutrients can have mild to severe health problems that often times can be gotten under control or even cured with a proper diet or nutrient supplements.

A study of 615 children in California in 1991 proves the powerful effect of nutrients on the mind. These children were given a nutrient supplement consisting of several key vitamins and minerals for twelve weeks. One-third of the students increased their IQ by ten points. This study also suggests that although children may seem to function just fine mentally and show no outward signs of being nutrient deficient, it's possible that they may not be reaching their potential mental capacity. It's often not until obvious mental symptoms appear that tests are done to determine if the cause is some type of nutritional deficiency. **The formula used by the researchers in the California study was:**

- vitamin A, 5,000 IU
- vitamin B1, 1.7 mg
- vitamin B2, 1.7 mg
- vitamin B3, 20 mg
- vitamin B5, 10 mg
- vitamin B6, 2 mg
- vitamin B12, 6 mcg
- vitamin C, 60 mg
- vitamin D, 400 IU
- vitamin E, 30 IU
- vitamin K, 50 mcg
- biotin, 300 mcg
- folic acid, 400 mcg
- calcium, 200 mg
- chromium, 100 mcg
- copper, 2 mg
- iodine, 150 mcg
- iron, 18 mg
- magnesium, 80 mg
- manganese, 2.5 mg
- molybdenum, 250 mcg
- selenium, 100 mcg
- zinc, 15 mg

Brain Boosting Nutrients Can Work for Anyone

People from all walks of life have experienced the power of nutrients to increase their mental stamina and allow them higher levels of thinking, concentration, and memory. Writers taking nutrients like choline, ginkgo biloba, ginseng, and others often talk about how they seldom experience writer's block like they used to.

People with highly technical jobs like chemists and computer programmers have been documented as saying they are able to retain more information as they work on multi-faceted projects.

You might know of people yourself who swear to the benefits of taking one or more of the vitamins, minerals, herbs, or other source of brain boosting nutrients. Maybe you even noticed a difference in their speech, trains of thought, short and/or long term memory, or overall mood.

An Introduction to Smart Drugs

Along with the knowledge that science has obtained about the brain boosting benefits of many kind of nutrients, science has recently developed and continues to test what is referred to as "smart drugs."

Smart drugs are new on the supplement market, having only been introduced since the early 1980s. They are still considered experimental and have not been approved by the U.S. Food and Drug Administration. Yet, they are available for purchase through specialty distributors. You can even order "smart" drinks at some juice cocktail bars found around the U.S. A smart drink is most often your favorite health juice, like carrot or celery, that has one or more smart drugs added to it. Typically these drinks will also include a several of the known brain boosting vitamins, minerals and amino acids, plus either phenylaline or choline (or both).

The verdict on the safety of smart drugs is still out, but they seem to be safe in moderate amounts. They work by providing the brain with a generous supply of oxygen.

Although adequate supplies of oxygen are absolutely necessary for the healthy functioning of the brain, oxygen is also the source of free radicals. Smart drugs are not only able to bring large amounts of oxygen to the brain, they are also very effective at ridding the brain of excess free radicals that may be generated as a result. They are also effective at ridding the brain of other kinds of toxins and cellular debris.

An introduction to the six smart drugs is listed below:
Smart Drug #1: Piracetam

Piracetam is what's known as a nootropic, meaning "acting on the mind." Most smart drugs are considered nootropic. Piracetam is also often referred to as Nootropil. It was first developed in Belgium, and is said to wake up your brain. It is a synthesized drug that resembles the structure of an amino acid known as pyroglutamate. Pyroglutamate is said to have the following properties:

- speed up the flow of information between the left and right brain hemispheres
- boost brain function during times of low oxygen levels
- stimulate the growth of receptors in neurons
- improve memory
- increase the level of energy within the brain

People who have used piracetam have reported better moods, greater alertness, increased ability to think more broadly, better concentration, and the ability to better express themselves.

Smart Drug #2: Hydergine

The smart drug hydergine has been proven in studies to increase the brain's capacity in several ways as well as slow down the aging process. Hydergine is synthetically modeled after three alkaloids from a natural fungus found on rye grains. It is said to aid the brain in the following ways:

- increase memory, intelligence, and the ability to learn
- slow down the appearance of age pigments in the brain, thought to be associated with Alzheimer's disease
- boost brain function during times of low oxygen levels
- increase the supply of oxygen to the brain
- Increase the supply of blood to the brain
- rid the brain of free radicals and other toxins

Several studies have shown that hydergine is effective as an antisenility drug. Studies in Europe even suggest that hydergine can prevent and possibly reverse brain cell damage.

Smart Drug #3: DMAE

DMAE is a natural chemical that can be found in different kinds of fish like sardines and anchovies. This chemical can also be found in small amounts in your brain where it helps to increase acetylcholine levels. The theory is the more DMAE you have in your brain, the higher levels of acetylcholine you'll have as well to improve your overall brain function.

DMAE is probably one of the most popular and widely used smart drugs since it is considered a nutritional supplement can easily be found. It is able to give the entire nervous system a significant boost without any kind of "rush" feeling or a "crash" after its effects have worn off, which is often what happens with amphetamines.

Although the dosage recommended is between 250-1,000 mg daily, you will need to use it to find your own best level. Remember that too much DMEA can induce muscle tension, headaches, and insomnia.

Smart Drug #4: Vasopressin/Diapid

Vasopressin naturally occurs in your brain as a hormone released by the pituitary gland. It is necessary for memory. It aids the brain by taking in new information and making it "stick".

Vasopressin has shown to have the following benefits to the brain:
- improves memory, both short and long term
- aids memory function and increases learning ability for people with memory afflictions
- can protect the brain from memory loss due to a physical or chemical injury
- can help reverse the effects of amnesia
- improves overall concentration and recall

Vasopressin can be prescribed by a doctor in a prescription form known as Diapid. This drug is especially recommended for older people or patients showing symptoms of memory decline. Since it is also used to treat diabetes patients who have problems with frequent urination, many physicians may not be aware of its benefits as a memory enhancer.

Vasopressin often comes in a nasal spray. It should not be taken every day. Your system builds up a tolerance to this drug and it will not be as effective over time. It is best to take it when you need a mental boost, like before an important test or other situation in which you know your utmost concentration and ability to recall information is needed.

Smart Drug #5: Lucidril

Lucidril is effective in helping remove what's known as lipofuscin deposits in your brain. These deposits are essentially age pigmentations that form over time and are by-products that accumulate from normal cell metabolism.

Lipofuscin deposits suffocate the neurons as they build up in the brain. Mental decline results from the destruction of large amounts of neurons. Although this is all a natural part of the aging process, smart drugs like lucidril can help slow down the aging process and maintain mental clarity longer.

Lucidril helps the brain in these ways:
- repair damage done at the synapse (space between neurons)
- sharpen brain power in the elderly or those suffering from mental or memory impairments
- rejuvenate brain cells that have been damaged by the aging process

Lucidril acts quickly. Recommended dosage is between 1,000-3,000 mg daily. Many users of the drug notice stimulating effects almost immediately.

6. Smart Drug #6: DHEA

Like DMAE, DHEA is a naturally occurring hormone found in the body. It is highly concentrated in the brain, with levels at about 6.5 times more than anywhere else.

Levels of DHEA decline with age. Rather than have specific attributes and benefits, scientists believe DHEA acts to generally support many of the body's natural processes. It seems to be important in the manufacture of steroid hormones.

DHEA's benefit to the brain seems to be in its ability to improve memory and overall brain function. Studies suggest it works to keep neurons healthy and encourages the growth of new dendrites. Low levels of DHEA actually result in nerve degeneration.

DHEA is available through a prescription by your doctor. The dosage is between 25-100 mg.

Brain Building Exercises
1. Tracking
With your eyes, practice tracking moving objects. Increase your skill level and benefit to your brain by practicing this in a darkened room. You can use a flashlight suspended to the ceiling. Watch it swing back and forth. Or have a friend wave the flashlight around in the room. You can even move it around yourself. Follow the light as you create formations and shapes.

2. Hanging Upside Down

Hanging upside down delivers oxygen-rich blood to your brain. It also stimulates the areas of your brain that affect your spatial orientation and help you balance. If you can stand on your head, you can practice this exercise in your own home. This exercise is easy to practice when swimming. Simply do headstands in the water. Or, you can hang upside down from vertical bars as are found on playgrounds, or on a rope hung vertically, or rings also hung for the purposes of swinging upside down.

3. Movie Movement

Watch the videos you rent or the movies you see at the theater with new eyes. Try to keep one step ahead of the plot and events before they unfold: What will happen next to the main character? How will the dilemmas that are building be solved? How does the plot move from phase to phase to build on itself? What details are particularly important for the forward movement of the movie? What works and what doesn't?

Adventure dramas and mysteries particularly add spice to this game. Watch for all the little details that add to heighten the suspense or mystery. Also look for the details that give you clues into what will happen next, i.e., cause and effect.

Your brain benefits from mental exercises that cause you to think deeply, hold your concentration, and challenge it to make connections between information and stimuli. Strengthening your brain in this way is not only good for building your overall brain power, but is fun while you're doing it as well.

Chapter 4
The Rhythms of the Brain

Scientists who study the brain while it sleeps long ago discovered that the brain actually goes though several different and distinct phases during every night of slumber.

It turns out that the brain has rhythms which come and go on a regular basis.

There are four phases of sleep: Stage 1, Stage 2, also known as REM sleep. REM stands for "rapid eye movement. It is during this phase which people dream. The next is Stage 3, and Finally Stage 4, also known as Delta Sleep, the deepest, most remote phase of the sleep cycle.

Each stage of sleep come about an fairly regular intervals, which change throughout the night. About 90 minutes after you go to sleep, you are very likely to enter REM stage and have your first dream. You will remain in REM sleep for only a few minutes and move on to Stage 3.

As the night goes on, REM sleep stays longer and longer. By morning, you may be dreaming just about all the time. If you think about it, you probably have realized that you have most of your dreams, and your most vivid dreams.

Some people think they never dream, but this is not the case. Studies in laboratories have proved conclusively that every person dreams every night, whether they know it or not. Those who think they never dream simply are not remembering their dreams.

Scientists were astonished when they first discovered the rhythmic patter of the sleeping brain. It had always been assumed that the brain function in only one way, or in one particular mode. The only differentiation to brain function thought to exists before sleep research was that the brain was at times "more active" than at other times.

It wasn't long before the revelations about the night rhythms of the brain led to speculation that perhaps the brain moved in rhythms during its waking hours as well. After all, who hasn't experienced that time of day when you just feel 'blah' and all you can think about is stretching out for a nice nap. At other times, you feel in peak mental form as you perform your work, read difficult material or breeze through a tough exam. Why do we find it easy to ace an exam sometimes, and struggle at others, even though we studied and prepared the same way for each test?

At least part of the answer lies in brain rhythms — at certain times of day, your brain is functioning at peak efficiency, while at others, it would be better if you were resting your brain by napping or perhaps working out the rest of your body in a gym. Sometimes, the brain is just not in rhythm to work. When you attempt critical thinking, problem solving and other mental gymnastics during the times when your brain is in "low rhythm" you are working against yourself, rather than "going with the flow" of your natural brain rhythms. Thinking hard when your brain is at low rhythm ebb is liking trying to run a marathon when you have just spent the last several hours digging a ditch. It's time to rest, not do more!

While it's true that life does not always afford us the luxury of working when we feel like it and resting when we feel like it, there is still much to be gained by working with your brain rhythms rather than against them. In many cases, you can plan and organize your day around those times when you are having peak brain performance, and those times when it would make sense to rest the brain with either naps or physical-oriented, nonthinking activity, such as exercise or meditation.

But before you can do any of this, you need to know more about brain rhythms, how they flow, how long they last and how you can tune them to optimum performance.

First, you must learn to monitor your own feelings, performance and attitudes throughout the day. Are there any clues which point to a low-ebb time of brain rhythm? The answer is yes. Here are 12 "Signals" which you can monitor in your own self.

They tell you when your brain is ready for a break:

- You suddenly yawn and feel a strong desire to stretch.

- A slight tingling or numbness in your extremities — toes, fingers, scalp or even elbows.

- You catch yourself in a sudden day dream. One minute you're working, the next you're thinking: "Wouldn't it be fun to vacation in Iceland?" A definite sign your brain wants to just relax and wander!

- You began to feel intuitive, rather than analytical. In other words, you start getting gut feelings, rather than wrestling problems to the ground with your critical thinking ability.

- You become sleepy and "dreamy" feeling.

- You crave a sweet snack (remember, the brain uses only sugar!)

- Feelings of bliss or happiness began to glow within you.

- You feel clumsy, slow or groggy.

- You become sick and tired of working. You can't wait for lunch break, a walk or time away from what you are doing.

- You have a strong desire to change what you are doing.

- You have an urge for a change of scenery.

- If you work at a desk job, you pick up a pen and start doodling while your mind wanders; you absentmindedly play with the keys at the keyboard; you sit back in your chair and stare into space — If you work at a job of physical labor, you find yourself staring at your tape measure while not really reading it; you trace patterns in the dirt with your work boot; you tilt your face into the sun to feel the warmth on your face.

Whatever your work situation, signs of low brain activity favor nonfocused, dreamy and intuitive patterns, while high brain activity favor a focused mind that is "100 percent here" and sharply within the present moment.

So, you recognize the signs of low-brain rhythm. What do you do? Most brain researchers agree: you're best off taking a 15-20 minute break.

Again, many of you may say: "Hey, I've got a job to do! I can't just clock out and meditate or day dream for 20 minutes at my desk. My boss would hand me my walking paper if he saw me doing it enough times!"

This might be true, and we must deal with reality. Don't get yourself fired! But listen: your brain is the product of millions of years of evolution. Its patterns and rhythms have been established and shaped over countless centuries. Working against it is just not smart Working with your brain IS smart, no matter what the time clock at your job demands of you.

Many employers are beginning to recognize that rigid, artificial patterns of when to work and when to rest do not automatically spell peak performance or production from their employees. Many workplaces are becoming more flexible, allowing employees to work at their own pace and on their own time — as long as the work that needs to get done indeed gets done!

Also, many of you have a job wherein you can select your own work patterns as you please. If you can't perhaps it's time to seek a new job.

Are we kidding? No! The days of slavery are over. And the days of wage slavery should be over as well. Just because someone is paying you to be somewhere and do something for 40 hours a week does not mean that you owe them the allegiance of your entire being. Sometimes, getting into sync with your life — and in this case your brain — means making radical changes in your total lifestyle. We'll talk more about total lifestyle changes later in this book.

Don't quit your job today. Try some adjustments first. All we are saying is that if your place of employment is so rigid and constricting, it's probably doing you more harm than the good your pay check is bringing into your life. Those who break out of whatever constrictive shells they are bound within find it easier to shape the kind of life they want around them, putting in order a life that works with the brain, mind and spirit, rather than plundering it crassly for labor and the gain of others.

Many employers these days still treat the human being like another office machine. They want it to function when the time is right for them, and they want to shut it off when the time is right for them. Like a machine, they expect you to turn yourself "on" and 8 a.m. to commence working and "off" at 4:30 p.m. when you can go home. They allow you to turn yourself off for two 15-minute periods during each day, but those time slots are strictly controlled and monitored by the time clock.

For millions of years, the human brain has tuned itself to work within the rhythms of the seasons, the sunlight and darkness, the temperature of the air, the availability of the kinds of foods — and now we expect the brain to act like the simplest of Xerox machines, following the arbitrary pattern of the 8-hour work day as set by modern, corporate, industrial society.

Every 90 to 120 minutes, the human body moves through a rhythm that involves the division of cells, the replication of genes, the replication of chromosomes, hormone production, hormone secretion and regulation, neurotransmitter release in the brain, and so forth.

You have peaks and valleys of performance, both in the body and the brain. All of your functions are affected. Your memory, your ability to solve problems, your ability to make intuitive or creative leaps, your reflexes, your hand-to-eye coordination, anything you can think of that goes on in your body — it all functions at peak efficiency at some moments, and would rather not function at all other times.

Even a genius like Albert Einstein experienced times when his brain did not seem to function at it's brilliant best. In fact, Einstein reported that he needed 10 hours of sleep every night. If he got anything less than that, he felt groggy and unable to function properly. The point is, you're human too. You may be smart (maybe even as brilliant as Albert!) but even you will have "down times" as far as your brain is concerned. Even a genius is an idiot sometimes!

You could become more like a genius in your every day life if you would work with the patterns of your brain, rather than fighting against it.

Now, above we told you the 12 signs that your brain may be signalling that it's going into low ebb. The brain cycle is headed for a valley. What do you do next? How can you best make use of your time when your brain would like to take a back seat to recharge?

Of course, the first thing you should do is STOP! Stop trying to force feed critical thinking tasks through your brain! It doesn't want to do that now! It's time to switch gears and let the mind go where it will. There is a saying in Zen: "The best way to control a cow is to give it a very large pasture."

In other words, the more you try to force your brain to think sharply and critically, the more it is going to go wrong, break out of the fence, make a mistake and just fumble around. A brain at low ebb needs a very large pasture in which it does not have to worry about the narrow rigid constraints of a fence — in this case, the rigors of the heavy thinking you want it to do.

You must tell yourself that it okay to stop pushing things right now, and relax. In fact, this step is critical. You must affirm to yourself that relaxation is not only okay, but necessary for peak performance. Much of what causes us to go against the grain is needless guilt. We are programmed to guard against "slacking," "sandbagging, "lollygagging," or whatever term you want to go with. Because of this, we feel that we should be working as hard as we can, as long as we can, and that we are to take breaks only during designated break times.

But let's look at it this way: the objective of your job is maximum productivity. If you take into account that a break will result in a temporary slowdown, but a long term increase in production, then the net result of a brain break is in the best interest of maximum productivity.

So now that you have recognized that your brain wants to take a break, and that you have accepted the fact that taking a break is in the best interest of maximum productivity, it's time to make the best of your down time.

The brain usually requires at least 15 minutes to begin its cycle back toward peak performance, but 20 minutes is more likely. So set your brain break relaxation time for at least 15 minutes, with 20 minutes being better.

Next, get comfortable someplace. You may simply lean back in the chair you are sitting in. It would be better to get up, walk around and change location. Many people take this kind of opportunity to have a cigarette break. The tobacco break is an extremely bad idea if your intention is maximum brain rejuvenation. As we have explained elsewhere and at length in this book, cigarettes tend to deteriorate and inhibit brain function, especially over the long term, rather than give your brain a chance to take in more badly needed clean, fresh oxygen.

But get up and move around. You may want to lie down, if not for a nap, but a session of blissful "free-mind" time; that is, just let go of your thoughts completely and watch them go by. You must get comfortable with doing nothing. Many people who take breaks think they need to being doing something "productive" in this time as well.

One woman said she "takes it easy" by listening to books on tape during her break from her job as a telephone sales representative. This might be exactly the right thing to do, or not a good thing to do at all. It depends on what kind of break her brain is really looking for. Most likely, her brain does not want to leave on task requiring focused attention, only to be yoked up into another task of forced attention. Listening to a book, following the plot, thinking about the characters, trying to visualize the scenery of a book is not exactly a break from the standpoint of the brain. On the other hand, perhaps an escape into the fantasy world of a good novel is exactly the escape the brain is looking for. Perhaps the job of being a telephone representative leaves little to the imagination centers of the brain, and the brain may crave to exercise this portion of its matrix.

How do you tell if one kind of break is a "good" brain break, and another is a "bad" brain break? Simply by how you feel when the 20-minutes is over. Do you feel focused an energized, or does getting back to the tasks at hand seem like more of a drag than ever? If the latter is the case, you are taking the wrong kind of brain break.

We believe the "can't go wrong" brain break is the "do nothing" break, where you simply let your mind loose and do nothing with it. The mind considers a long meandering walk through the endless and timeless fields of consciousness to be the true release it needs from constantly being asked to focus, concentrate, think critically, analytically, objectively and with as little error as possible.

This goes against the thinking of the average person in America today. Most of us were raised with a strong work ethic in which "the devil finds use for idle hands." To simply do nothing engenders a feeling of guilt, if not an an itchy feeling that says: "do anything — just move!" This is all well and good. Hard work is what makes a person wealthy and is what makes this country great, but the time has come for our society to look beyond wealth and success. We must also remember the human condition and the place for the individual amid all this wealth and progress that our work produced. If our work is meant simply to produce only more work, progress may continue, but a certain emptiness creeps into the progress, and people end up feeling alienated, tired and permeated with a sense of meaninglessness — like a hamster running on a wheel in a cage, endlessly chasing a bit of food it can never catch.

The answer is not to stop working, and not to stop progress, but to simply find little spaces of quiet within all the work and clamor of our daily lives. We all need an oasis that we can simply step onto no matter where we are. We need to set up an automatic bubble of silence and peace. In this serene environment, we can release our brains from their endless bondage and demands for them to work on and on forever.

And here's the way to think about doing nothing: DOING NOTHING IS ACTUALLY PRODUCTIVE! That's right! Scientific studies show that regular breaks in which people do nothing but sit, lie down or just let their mind go where it will return to work and are able to work at a much more efficient rate. The greater work efficiency rate afforded by the "nothing break" more than makes up for the few minutes of lost time when the worker is doing nothing. It's all because this kind of practice takes advantage of the natural rhythm of the brain.

Rather than forcing the brain to work when it does not want to, giving it a "free space" recharges it quickly and makes it come back better than ever. Another bonus of a brain break: it cuts down on error rates at work, or any situation. THAT'S ANOTHER WAY DOING NOTHING IS ACTUALLY PRODUCTIVE! Often, the errors made during times of low brain function can rob or even erase hours of productivity that came before it. When you look at it this way, a do nothing brain break is not doing nothing at all — it's a little insurance policy that not only prevents and reduces worker error, but increases productivity.

Remember that when you are giving your brain a do nothing break — do just that — NOTHING! This might seem simple, but ask anyone who takes up meditation for the first time. It's extremely difficult! In a particular kind of meditation   Zen Meditation — the object is to not only do nothing, but to THINK nothing. The goal is to completely forget everything, even your own thoughts. Ask any experienced Zen meditator, and they'll tell you it takes years upon years to reach the "no mind" state of being.

Please remember that meditation is not necessarily a religious exercise. It is not associated exclusively with eastern religions, such and Zen Buddhism, the Sufi sects of Islam, the Yogi masters of India, or others. Meditation is not something only people involved in cults or esoteric eastern religions do. There are many forms of Christian meditation, as well as meditation techniques that have nothing to do with religion what-so-ever.

Just because you decide to practice meditation does not mean you have to abandon your current religion, nor does it mean you are doing anything that is "weird" or somehow philosophically unwholesome. Meditation is safe for anyone to practice. Meditation does not involve going into a trance, or putting yourself in a state of mind that will make you passive, or open to unwanted mental intrusions from negative sources.

Meditation also does not involve sitting in an uncomfortable, contorted position on the floor, burning incense or chanting — unless you choose to do those things.

Simply put, meditation merely involves sitting quietly, clearing your mind of troubles and turmoil, and seeking a feeling of peace and center.

How to meditate

So now that we have done away with some of the myths of meditation, let's try it out.

Meditation can be incredibly simple, yet deceptively difficult at times. The whole trick of meditation (if there is a trick at all) is to sit or lie down quietly and release everything from your mind, whether it be positive or negative thoughts.

Try this:

Find a chair in a quiet room where there are no other people, no television or radio playing, and no other distractions.

Sit in your chair, but don't sit like you usually do. Sit closer to the edge of the chair. Put your feet flat on the floor, and keep your back straight. Put your hands palms down on your knees. You should be able to draw a straight line from the bottom of your spine, up through your back, neck and the back of your head — and the line would be perpendicular with the ceiling. Don't try to be too stiff, as if a metal rod has been rammed down your spine. Just keep yourself generally straight, as if your were trying to practice good posture.

The next thing you want to do is take three slow, deep breaths. As you inhale imagine that you are drawing positive energy into your body, and as you exhale, imagine that all pain and negativity is rushing out of your body. Do it anyway you want. Some people like to imagine a stream of golden, positive energy entering their body as they inhale, and black or gray negative energy leaving their body as they exhale. But it's really up to you how you want to visualize this. It's usually best to invent your own way.

After doing three big breaths, you will probably notice that your mind is more quiet and more focused, that your heart rate is more steady, and you are feeling more calm.

The next thing you want to do is to simply see how long you can maintain this peaceful mental state, concentrating on your breathing, and keeping your mental activity to a minimum. The first day, try for 5 minutes and eventually work your way up to 10 minutes per session.

An important tip: Don't try to hard to keep your mind clear and calm. The harder you try, the more difficult you will find it to keep you mind empty. You will find that all kind of thoughts will persistently intrude on your attempt to remain calm and empty. It's incredibly difficult to let go of the million things we all have to think about each day —

but that's the whole purpose of meditation — to give yourself a break from the daily chatter in your mind.

Don't worry, it's only for ten minutes. You can go back to whatever thoughts or worries you wish after your meditation session has been completed. But for just this ten minutes, once per day, commit yourself to a calm mind.

And at this point you might be thinking: How could anything so simple and uncomplicated really do me any good, especially for only 5 to 10 minutes per day?

But the facts are — and there is an enormous amount of medical data to back this up — that meditation can do everything from lower your blood pressure, to cure cancer, heal your heart, lower your cholesterol level, ease your addictions and much more.

Meditation is widely regarded by those inside and outside the medical community as one of the most powerful tools available for both preventative health care, and for easing existing conditions. Because most of our lives are so fast-paced, and so filled with endless stress and activities, the precious ten minutes you give yourself once a day may be the very oasis of sanity that will allow your body to catch up and strengthen itself against the daily onslaught of the fast-paced American lifestyle, which most of us face everyday.

To sum up: To meditate you need to remember only four basic things:

1) Find a quite, undisturbed place where you can be alone for 10 minutes without distractions.

2) Sit in a comfortable, upright posture, with back straight and face forward, hands on your knees. You may also lie flat on your back with hands at your sides or on your stomach.

3) Concentrate on your breathing while ignoring all your other thoughts. Note: it is extremely important that you don't try to "fight off" your thoughts. This will only make them louder and more persistent. Just let them run past you — let your mind flow like a stream, a stream which you pay little attention to.

4) Do it at least once a day, although a ten minute session in the morning and an equal one at might will bring optimum results.

You've done it!

That's all there is to it! If you practice this simple meditation once or twice a day, you may start noticing results in your daily life and general level of health immediately.

If you don't get immediate results, stick with it for two weeks. If by then you can still say meditation has done you no good, then you've wasted little time, and you'll know this stuff is not for you.

By the way, this and other kinds of meditation does more than recharge your brain power,it may even help keep you young. That's right! People who meditate on a regular basis live longer than those that don't. Furthermore, thcy don't just live longer, they look younger and feel younger.

According to a study reported in the Journal of Behavioral Medicine, people who meditate on a regular basis have levels of age-related hormones that are comparable to those of meditaters five to 10 years younger.

A hormone with the mouthful name of dehydroepaindosterone sulfate (DHEA-S) is produced by the adrenal gland. The rate at which it is produced normally increases through the early 20s, then begins to decline.

In the study, the level of DHEA-S of 423 meditators were compared to that of 1,252 health nonmeditators. The subjects were divided into groups according to their age, and meditators were compared to nonmeditators in the same age proximity.

Meditating females showed higher DHEA-S levels than nonmeditating women in every age group. Men under age 40 showed little variation, but after age 40, meditators began to show significantly higher levels of the youth hormone that nonmeditators.

We're not saying that you have to achieve the refined state of mind attained by the Zen Master's, but you must let go and resist your urge to do something — anything. Just simply sit and be. Don't go watch TV. Don't listen to music. Don't read an interesting magazine article. You want your brain to be completely free for a time period so it can rest itself without any distractions of any kind. This time period optimally is 20 minutes. Shorter than that time may not be enough, and longer may get you out of the work mode entirely. Remember your goal: to recharge your brain with nothing so that you can go back to doing something.

When it's time to go back to work, you will find doing so is a lot easier. You may not only be surprised at how much better work goes, you may be stunned! Your brain is suddenly rapping out on all cylinders again. You accomplish difficult tasks with greater ease. You find it easier to get absorbed in your work and you are less prone to distraction. You see, if you let your brain know that it is going to have times when it can be free to be and do nothing, it automatically works better when it's time to accomplish something.

Some people may find it a tad difficult to shift from brain-rest-do-nothing time, and back into word mode. Don't force it. Start easily by focusing your eyes on something outside yourself, preferably a work-related object or scene. Draw yourself into that scene or pick up that object. Tell yourself inwardly that it's time to work. Most of the time your brain will respond quickly and you'll be back at better than ever. If you don't find yourself jumping back in, you may need more rest than you thought. If you can, give it another five minutes, or 10 maximum. Then get out there and get back on the horse whether you feel ready to go or not.

For those of you who feel like you want to stay in the "do nothing" phase, perhaps it's time for you take a look at the big picture. You made need an entire vacation. You may need something even more drastic — like a change of job, or some extended time off from any and all kinds of work. Now we're not saying that taking a do nothing break is going to make everyone suddenly lose interest in their jobs and make them run off to Tahiti for a life of carefree traveling and adventure. (Sorry, didn't mean to make that sound too good!) But a certain and small percentage of people are far more caught up in their daily lives of work and stress than they know. As you are reading this, there are literally thousands of people who are far, far too stressed out, far, far too much in need of a long vacation or major change in not only their work, but entire lifestyle. Did you know that the majority of all heart attacks happen to men between the hours of 8 and 9 o'clock Monday morning? This is a very telling statistic. It means that thousands of men are literally ready to die rather than start another long week of non-stop work stress and unrelenting demands upon their minds and brain. Rather than take more, the body takes over control from the brain, unleashes a heart attack so that things can come to an extended halt. It's a drastic step to be sure, but sometimes the risk of death is better than another week of stressful hell at the workplace.

For a person like this, a brain break may be the very thing that saves his or her life. Such a person may be the kind who does not feel like going back to work even after 20 or 30 minutes. If this is you, it's time for some deep introspection about your position in life and work. Don't do anything drastic. Rather, start to think about how you feel about your life and your work. It is time for a change? Is it time to slow down? Only you know the answers for yourself, but sometimes knowing the answer is not enough. You also need the courage to face the correct answer. Far too many people know they need a break or a change, but they simply do not have the courage to make the change. To often, the result is the body taking things into it's own hands, with a heart attack, a stroke or some other kind of physical or mental break down. You can prevent this from happening.

So a brain break is more than just a way to rejuvenate yourself and increase your productivity, it could be the safety valve that will save your life. That's a lot of value for a few minutes of simply doing nothing! And that's why you should never underestimate this very powerful brain boosting technique!

NOTES:

_____

_____

_____

_____

_____

_____

_____

_____

_____

_____

_____

_____

Chapter 5
Acupuncture –
The Key to the Brain?

Seven years ago while visiting his boyhood home in the wooded hills of southwestern Wisconsin, 55-year-old Warren L. of San Diego took a long broken slide down the side of a rocky bluff. He did not stop until 400 feet later. Bruised and scraped, but not seriously harmed, or so he thought, Warren brushed himself off and walked the two miles back home.

Warren had to catch a plane early the next day so when his alarm went off at 6 a.m. the next morning, he intended to jump out of bed, but to his amazement, the best he could manage was a slow, painful roll to the side of the bed. Every movement was agony. It took him another 10 minutes to sit up. Eventually, he got himself motivated enough to shower, dress and take a cab to the airport. But pain accompanied each movement he made, especially his back.

When he got off the plane in California his family immediately knew he was in pain by the way he hobbled across the airport floor. Although in his mid-50s, Warren was in excellent shape with a trim athletic body and very sharp mind. His work as a college professor and his two hobbies — running and rock climbing — kept both body and mind in peak shape.

But something in that fall back in Wisconsin took the edge off of Warren's physical condition. The next day he was in the doctor's office undergoing a battery of tests. They all revealed nothing. Warren's doctor told him to go home, get some rest, and his body would heal up on its own without further medical help, except for some pain killer to make things easier why he waited to heal.

He waited, but he did not heal. Warren's tremendous back pain continued. And although his doctor had sent him home with a bottle of Percodan, a powerful narcotic pain killer, Warren was not the kind of guy that liked to take pain pills that made him drowsy, and which also could be addictive.

After a couple weeks of suffering, Warren's 18-year-old daughter suggested he try acupuncture — the ancient Chinese art of healing with needles in the body. At first, Warren balked. After all, he was an educated man and did not believe is so called "nontraditional" or "alternative" medicine. Still, what did he have to lose? He was in pain. Mainstream medicine could do nothing for him except drug him into a stupor. Why not give the needles a whirl? he thought.

Warren did so. His daughter made an appointment for him with an acupuncturist of good reputation. Warren reclined down on a table and the acupuncturist inserted several needles at strategic points throughout his body. Within 15 minutes of having the needles placed in his body, Warren was amazed to feel his pain melt away, as if it had been turned off like a switch.

Warren, a former skeptic, became as instant believer in this ancient healing technique. He still did not know how it worked. He only know it did work. Warren decided to apply his well-educated mind to a search for answers. He wanted to know how a few needles placed in seemingly random parts of the body could make pain disappear - the same pain modern medicine had no good answer for.

Warren's research took him to a closer study of the human nervous system, especially the human brain. In this chapter, like Warren, we are going to take a closer look at how acupuncture affects the human brain, and explore how it can not only heal pain, but supercharge your brain to make it function better, faster and with greater clarity.

4000 Years of Healing

No one knows for sure when the Chinese came up with the idea to stick needles in people as a way to stop pain and heal, but most put the beginning of the practice back 4,000 years or more. And even though we have had 40 centuries of experience with acupuncture, how it works remains a mystery to this very day.

Most ancient texts explain acupuncture in terms of an energy which is said to "flow" through the human body. This energy goes by many names, but most call it "chi," which is pronounced "chee." Some spell it Qi. This vital energy is what moves or animates the body, including the flow of blood and muscle movements. The ancients also gave chi credit for protecting the body from disease and for keeping it warm. Some ancient healers even claimed the ability to see the chi glowing around the human body like an aura. Many alternative healers claim the same ability today, and some even perform "aura adjustments." But that's a whole other topic. Suffice it to say that the idea that the body contains some kind of fundamental energy or power is part of many beliefs and had been for centuries.

Whenever this vital force is "clogged up" or disrupted from flowing through the body in a regular pattern, the result is disease and pain. Especially important are certain "power points" identified at various locations in the body. If one of these power points in disrupted, closed down or just not functioning right, a lot of things go wrong with the body. It does not always have to be disease or pain. Vital force disruption can also mean a lack of energy, weight gain, feelings of sluggishness, or even mental problems, like depression and anxiety.

The theory of acupuncture is that sticking needles into these specific power points can be a way of stimulating them back into functioning properly. If one is closed, the needle can open it again. If energy is not flowing properly, the stimulation of the needle causes the energy to start flowing again like it should again. Once the energy flow is restored to its proper manner, the body can not only return to health, but thrive and be energized.

How many power points are there throughout the body? Well, experienced acupuncture professionals identify as many as 1,500. And what's interesting about these power points is the fact that they don't necessarily have any logic of locational connection to the part of the body they are supposed to control, or serve. For example, sticking a needle behind the big toe is said to affect the functioning of the brain. The toe is as about as far away from the brain as you can get on the human body! But just as we saw in the section about reflexology, there are indeed recognized nerve endings in the big toe that lead directly back to the brain. Thus, plucking these nerve strings sends a message directly back to the brain, and can have a powerful effect on the workings of the brain. Like the pressure applications of reflexology, needles that tweak specific power points of the body seem to be extremely good ways to produce positive results.

More good evidence to suggest that point out on the body lead directly to the brain are experiments in which pins were stuck into eye-related acupuncture points in the feet. After doing so, brain monitors indicated that areas of the brain's visual cortex lighted up and increased its electrical activity.

Opposite Forces

In addition to the concept of a life force or vital energy is the concept of forces that oppose each other so that they can balance each other. You may have heard of the Chinese terms, "yin and yang." The yin is said to represent the female force and the yang the male force. Other traditions do not make a distinction based on gender values, but suffice it to say that there are two different kinds of forces in the body that must work together in a cooperative manner for everything to be "okay" with the body.

People suffering from "yin conditions" show a lack of chi, such as paleness, chills, slow pulse, depression, lack of energy — sort of an anemic state of existence. Those with a "yang condition" are said to display the opposite: fever instead of cold, rapid pulse instead of slow, nervousness or hyperactivity instead of sluggishness and redness or flushed skin instead of being pale.

Once again, it is the application of needles to specific power points that can balance a yin condition back toward yang, or a yang back toward yin, and ultimately create a perfect balance between the two in the human body.

Every year, licensed acupuncture specialists and even many medical doctors administer an amazing 15 million acupuncture treatments per year in the United States and Canada combined. The more it is used and the more success stories that result from it's application, the more the mystery and aura of "alternative or flaky" drops away from this method of treating human pain and suffering.

Today, modern western science finally seems to be catching up to ancient healing arts like acupuncture. Modern medicine now has tools that can shed light on all of this, including on how acupuncture works, especially on how it works on the human brain. That's important, since your brain is the organ that processes feelings of pain. Pain is in the brain, so to speak. If the brain pain centers can be blocked without drugs, and instead with the painless insertion of a few needles, it gives healers a powerful way to bring relief people that are hurting, WITHOUT resorting to the harmful and addictive side effects of narcotics, such as codeine, morphine and other such substances.

Scientists so far have been able to prove that acupuncture affects the flow of a very important class of brain chemicals called endorphines. It works this way: when a needle is inserted into muscle tissue the nerves underlying that tissue is stimulated. That stimulation sends impulses up the spinal cord to a part of the brain known as the limbic system. The limbic system is often called the "primitive" part of the brain because it controls some of the more basic functions of the body, and no so-called "higher thought" occurs there. Just above the limbic system is the mid-brain, which we talk about frequently in other parts of this book. In the midbrain is the all important pituitary gland.

When a nerve is stimulated by an acupuncture needle, endorphines and another class of substances called "monoamines" are released into the limbic system and midbrain. The effect is the blockage of pain. Scientists now consider it a documented fact that acupuncture release endorphins and monoamines into the limbic system and midbrain, taking this aspect of acupuncture firmly out of the realm of mystical magic.

But the release of endorphins and monoamines in the brain does not explain how acupuncture helps with other kinds of illnesses, such as nausea and depression. Even such things as vision problems and hearing loss respond well to acupuncture treatment, and even the memory and intelligence can apparently be improved by these amazing little needles.

There is an entire area of power points which run along the outside of the foot, from the little toe to the ankle. This area of power points is sometimes called the "vision run."

To help prove that acupuncture needles are actually producing all the effects on the brain we have been talking about, scientists recently conducted studies of acupuncture treatment using the cutting edge technology of a medical machine called the MRI.

The MRI, or Magnetic Resonance Imager, is a machine in which a substance is placed in a strong magnetic field that affects the spin of the atomic nuclei of certain isotopes of common elements. A radio wave passes through the substance then reorients these same nuclei. When the wave is turned off, the nuclei release a pulse of energy that provides information on the molecular structure of the substance — and most importantly, all this can be transformed into an image by certain computer techniques.

In the early 1980s, the MRI became a diagnostic tool for obtaining more accurate and precise images of tissues within the human body than are possible with other advanced medical machines, such as the CAT scan and ultrasonics. Furthermore, in its medical applications, MRI does not involve radioactivity and ionizing radiation, but instead uses only electromagnetism to look at the brain and other body parts in a three-dimensional picture. Because of this, the MRI is the very best and most effective when used as an imaging technique for scans of the brain, head, and neck.

The MRI is also able to measure minute changes in the amount of oxygen carried in the blood. This is important because it is also something of a measure of how much glucose is being absorbed by muscle and other body tissues. Knowing how much oxygen and glucose in being carried to a particular body tissue is in turn a good measurement of how active it is.

One day, some innovative scientists came up with this brilliant idea: "Why not hook up a patient to an MRI machine while he or she is being given acupuncture stimulation and see what happens in the brain while this is being done? If something significant is discovered, it could not only unlock the secrets of acupuncture, but lead to even greater discoveries as to how to ease pain and make the brain function more efficiently.

In one such test, doctors stimulated those acupuncture points which correspond to the functioning of the eyes and sight. These points are located on the outside of the foot, and also on the urinary bladder meridian, which runs from a position near the top of the back shoulder down the body, down the leg to a point just above the ankle. There are several dozen points along this line.

To make the test more accurate, scientists first tried to stimulate the eyes directly, and without acupuncture. They flashed light directly into a subject's eyes to stimulate the eye into sending signals to the brain. The result is just what they expected — the image of the brain lighted up in that part which controls eye function. This area is known as the visual cortex.

Next, the poked a power point on the foot or on the urinary bladder meridian line — and the very same area of the brain — the visual cortex — lighted up, just as if the eye itself had been directly stimulated.

Scientists were amazed that sticking a needle in the outside area of the foot had the same effect on the brain as stimulating the eye directly with light. Furthermore, the needles were just as good at stimulating the visual cortex as was direct stimulation of the eyes. In other words, the acupuncture point was everything the healers of ancient China have always said it has been — a direct pathway to the functioning of the brain.

Next, the scientists tried other points — for speech, hearing, memory and intellect. And each time when a needle was stuck into the specific power point designated by ancient tradition, the brain scan responded in kind, showing clear stimulation of that region of the brain.

But then the researchers noticed something odd. In some cases when a specific area of the brain was activated, some showed an increase in oxygen and glucose activity, while others show a decrease. Why did some needle stimulation cause an increase in oxygen and glucose flow, while others caused a decrease in oxygen and blood flow? The answer again comes from ancient Chinese tradition — the difference in yin and yang. It turns out that people who had been identified as being yang by the acupuncturist showed an increase in activity while those that were identified as yin showed a corresponding decrease. Once again, the tenets of the ancient practice of acupuncture were confirmed and found to be consistent with modern scientific review.

These recent tests of the scientific and physiological accuracy of acupuncture have made many otherwise skeptical, mainstream doctors sit up and take notice of the potential for this practice to do some real good to people with real medical problems.

These studies and others caused the prestigious National Institute of Health to conclude that acupuncture is indeed an effective method for treating a great number of illnesses and pains. It is also help, the NIH said, in treated post surgical pain, the side effects of chemotherapy and nausea. The NIH was also forced to conclude that not only is acupuncture an effective treatment for all of the above, but that it is also equally effective as many of the medically scientific treatments for many major diseases and illnesses — and in some cases — is even better! That's because, unlike drugs which come with side effects, acupuncture is not a drug. It does not involve doping the blood with any foreign substances that can cause other problems for the patient — everything from addiction to liver damage.

Acupuncture is especially effective for treating chronic pain. In one study, researchers used something called SPECT, which stands for single photon emission computed tomography. This is a machine which records images of the brain which show blood flow to the brain structures that are suspected of releasing brain chemicals called endorphins, which we said earlier were known to ease pain and even produce sensations of pleasure in the human brain.

Comparing images of people who were in pain, and the same people after they received acupuncture treatment showed clearly that there was increased blood flow to those parts of the brain involved with the pain. More importantly, all the patients who were treated with acupuncture reported that they felt less pain. The latter report is worth more than all of the scientific data combined!

These studies go a long way toward showing that the effects of acupuncture are not psychological as many doctors have claimed, but rather, real pain relief based on actual physical changes in the brain.

What's exciting is acupuncture's potential to solve diseases of the brain, including Alzheimer's, Parkinson's Disease, senile dementia, poor memory, or just plain old fuzzy thinking. Consider the following real life example:

Helen K. of Minneapolis was 67 years old, active and still working at her job as an accountant with a major firm in the Twin Cities.

But suddenly, Helen found herself making more errors than she ever had before. More and more, she would get the numbers wrong on some very important spread sheets in some very important situations. One of Helen's mental errors resulted in a $68,000 chunk of red ink for one of her firm's most important and long-term clients.

Needless to say, she was called out on the carpet by her boss. True, Helen's work had always been sharp and error-less in the 37 years she had worked with this particular company. And the natural conclusion to jump to was that, at age 67, Helen had finally lost a step.

Her boss, trying to be kind, said to her: "Helen, you've had a great career. you've served this company with honor and distinction for 37 years. But nobody goes on forever. Let's face it. You're past your retirement curve — most accountants retire five years before you do. Maybe it's time to just hang it up."

Hearing these words, Helen burst into tears. The worst part of it all was that she had no defense. She had made the errors. That was on her, without doubt. Still, Helen was not the kind of person to simply give up. And she refused to believe that just because her age was now 67 she had somehow magically lost all the skill, knowledge and talent she had accumulated over the years. Helen firmly believed that she still had a lot to offer. She also believed that her recent cloudy mental performance was an abberation — a temporary condition that could be treated and made to go away, if only she could find the right remedy.

Helen first considered visiting her regular medical doctor, except for one thing. She had a lifetime fear and mistrust of doctors. You see, Helen had nearly died once at the hands of a doctor. It was after the birth of her second child. For some amazing reason, the attending doctor allowed her to go home with a portion of the birthing material — the placenta — still inside of her. Within a day or two, the birthing material began to decay inside her body, leaching toxins into her system. She nearly died. Only an emergency surgery and a radical treatment with heavy antibiotics pulled her through. That was 40 years ago. She has never trusted a doctor since.

But now she was faced with a dilemma. Something was obviously wrong with her thinking process. Her mind was cloudy. Her memory was shaky. She was making mistakes at work. She needed help from somewhere. Luckily, it came from an unexpected source.

Helen's daughter, Minerva, the very same child she had almost died giving birth too suggested that her mother see an acupuncturist.

At first, Helen, ever the conservative accountant, balked. "You expect me to go to some kind of witch doctor so that he can stick pins all over my body! No way!"

But Miverva kept after her. She said: "Mom, listen! Acupuncture is no longer some kind of esoteric or mystical practice practiced in back allies or in some kind of voodoo parlor. A lot of hard scientific study has been done on acupuncture and it has been all but proven to be a viable and powerful form of medicine. Also, it does not hurt. The needles are extremely fine, almost as thin as a human hair. You can hardly tell you are being poked. It hurts a lot less than say, a flu shot, and the effect is a lot more powerful than any drug you can get from a doctor."

Minerva kept at Helen until she finally gave in. After all, she was scared. She may have been losing the most precious thing she had — her mind. Minerva set up an appointment, and in two days, Helen found herself in a place she never thought she would be — on the table of a professional acupuncturist.

Having described her problems to the acupuncturist, the practitioner began inserting needles at strategic points throughout Helen's body. Thankfully, Helen felt absolutely no pain. Furthermore, she also felt herself feeling strangely relaxed after the needles had been set. SHe even began to feel slightly joyful, and clear headed. Within a half hour, the treatment was done. Helen was scheduled to come in for two sessions a week for the next six weeks. Again, she felt she had nothing to lose, so she kept each appointment faithfully. In the meantime, after two weeks off, she returned to her place of work and begged her boss for another chance. She said to him:

"I've given the best 37 years of my life to this firm. I've never missed a day of work. I've always showed up on time and done good work. Yes, I've made some mistakes recently, but I was suffering from a temporary condition that caused me to loose certain aspects of my critical thinking. That's now in the past. I've never felt better, and I want to get back to work!"

Helen was telling the truth about her mental condition. The acupuncture had worked a seeming miracle on her brain. She suddenly began to feel more clear headed than she ever thought she could again. Something about the acupuncture treatment had put her vital bodily forces back in balance. Her brain and mind were now not only back to normal - they were better than ever before.

The acupuncturist told her that her vital force — her chi — was out of balance, but that the treatment had now put things back in order. He recommended further visits twice a year to make sure that everything remained healthy and balanced within her system.

Helen's boss didn't know what to say. The woman sitting in front of him was obviously no cloudy-minded senior citizen ready for a nursing home or a quiet game of shuffle board with the "oldy gang." He sensed that the "old Helen" was back — that is, the astute, sharp minded accountant who never missed a beat, and on several occasions, had saved the firm a pile of money.

Helen got her job back, and the rest is history. Today, Helen just celebrated her 70th birthday, and she has no plans to quit her job anytime soon.

Helen firmly believes she owes it all to acupuncture, the ancient, 4000-year-old Chinese art that has been helping sick people through the ages.

Helen's story proves that in addition to showing the ability to relieve pain and treat various diseases, acupuncture can very likely help healthy people become even healthier. One way it could do that is by stimulating the brain into a greater level of activity.

If you have a problem with your mind or thinking or memory, acupuncture may be your answer. Acupuncture is especially attractive to those who do not like to take drugs which can have unwanted side effects. Furthermore, acupuncture is painless, absolutely safe and has a mountain of data to back it up as a safe and effective treatment for the human body and the human brain.

So there you have it — one more resource to help make your brain the best and most healthy it can be.

Chapter 6
Drugs That Make You Smarter

In this chapter we're going to take an in-depth look at drugs that will not only make you smarter, but happier, more sexually fulfilled, more spiritual, and more focused and centered as a human being.

Can drugs do all of that? Well, remember that all consciousness is chemically based. By that we mean that, right now, the thoughts that are moving through your brain are being carried on the backs, so to speak, of brain chemicals — natural chemicals manufactured by your body to get the job of thinking done.

For example, when you think about and remember your wedding day, those images and sensations in your mind are encoded within the molecules of brain chemicals. When you look at a beautiful sunset, the images that flow through your eyes and optic nerves are transformed into images that your brain can "see." That vision is made up of brain chemicals. When you feel love for your child or another person, that feeling of love is chemically encoded. All this sounds a bit cold and clinical, but it really is not. Everything in your mind — all the good and all the bad together is made up of chemicals that can be identified in a laboratory setting.

Some examples of these chemicals are dopamine, L-Dopa, serotonin, endorphins, choline, and many, many more. These chemicals are manufactured by your brain. The point is, if our thoughts are made up of natural chemicals, that means we should be able to manipulate the brain by adding additional chemicals, both man-made substances and natural substances. We should be able to literally add specific kinds of thoughts by taking a pill. We should also be able to increase the efficiency of how we think.

Furthermore, if we can identify certain chemicals that make us happy and create feelings of pleasure — as do endorphins, for example — could we make a person even more happy by adding artificial endorphins to the bloodstream? Can we make a person smarter? Can we help people with brain degenerative diseases, such as Alzheimer's and Parkinson's Disease?

More and more, the answer to all of the above seems to be yes. More and more, scientists are getting excited over the promise of so-called "smart drugs." In this chapter, we are going to discuss the very latest development in smart drug research and explore exactly what they can do for you.

These days, the media seems very excited about smart drugs. Time Magazine recently devoted a cover story to the subject. ABC News With Peter Jennings does frequent stories about the latest developments in memory drugs, smart drugs, anti-brain aging drugs and more.

The idea has caught on, and if such major media outlets as Time and ABC news are paying attention, you can be sure of two things:
   (a) real scientific progress is being made in the field of smart drug development and
   (b) there is tremendous public interest in smart drugs, and tremendous public demand.

Everyone wants to be smarter. Better yet, people want to get smarter simply by taking a pill. Wouldn't it be great if you could boost your IQ 50 points simply by taking a pill every day the same way you take a vitamin? That beats spending four years in college, cramming your brain with facts and figures and training your brain to work better by working it harder.

If this sounds impossible, think about it a little deeper. For example, we already have "dumb drugs." One of the most prominent is alcohol, for example. When you put this chemical into your system, it automatically makes you dumber. Try doing your taxes when you're intoxicated on alcohol. The IRS may pay you a visit a short time later! Would you dare to take a college final exam while drunk? Obviously, alcohol is just one example of a drug that can make you temporarily dumber by impairing your overall brain function. Marijuana is another. Many scientific studies prove that marijuana inhibits short-term memory. A person with a weaker memory is a person who is less intelligent because he or she has one less mental tool to work with.

So we know that some drugs can make you dumb. If that's so easy, why not drugs that can make you smarter?

Again, there is already a great deal of evidence that even some very common substances make you smarter. One is good old coffee, or more specifically, the caffeine that's in the coffee. A recent study revealed that college students who drank coffee before a specific set of test performed an average of 13 percent better than those who did not have coffee or any other form of caffeine.

So caffeine is a "smart drug" of sorts. It clears your head, makes you more alert and basically makes thinking easier. The trouble is, caffeine is limited in it's ability to improve overall brain function. It gives you a little boost, clears you head, and perhaps make you do one in 10 tasks better or more efficiently But caffeine can't help you learn new tasks better or new subject matter better in an integral way. For example, if you already are poor at math, drinking a gallon of coffee a day will not help you get better at math. It will only make doing so a bit easier because you will be able to stay awake longer to study harder. But in this case, it is not the coffee making you smarter, but rather, you're studying. A real smart drug would do more than this.

A real smart drug would make you more intelligent across the board. A real smart drug should significantly improve your ability to learn difficult new material, such as math problems. A real smart drug should turn a math failure into a math success without any further effort on behalf of the subject. A smart drug should simply make your brain faster at grasping new concepts, should make your memory better, should make learning easier, and so on.

Some researchers dislike the name smart drugs because it gives the general public a wrong impression about what these kind of drugs are supposed to do. In general, today's smart drugs will not turn a flunky into an "A" student. Rather, they work to boost overall brain performance. Thus, some say the word "nootropics," from the Greek, meaning 'acting on the mind' is a much better word for the kind of drugs we are talking here. But since the term "smart drugs" has caught on, we'll continue to use the term in this chapter, although we may use nootropic as well. Just think of them as the same thing.

Many drugs can be labeled smart drugs, depending on how they are used and what for. To date, about 60 existing drugs fit the description of "smart drug." Most of these were originally developed not to make people smart, but to treat a disease of the brain, such as senile dementia. Others were created not for brain disease purposes at all, but to serve or correct an entirely different biological function, such as bladder control or stilling "the shakes." Thus, many drugs have come to be considered smart drugs because they only have side effects that enhance brain function. Most smart drugs today have been discovered by accident, you might say.

Many of the 60 drugs that are now considered smart drugs have actually been available and on the market for many years, some even decades. Also, many of the brain enhancing properties of these drugs have been known about for a long time. It just that, researchers have simply not considered the possibility of using drugs to enhance intelligence until about the mid-1980s. It's just not something that was done. There is a certain taboo about "messing with the mind. And medicine is primarily focused on "fixing negatives." For example, if a person is loosing his mental functions because of Alzheimer's Disease, doctors attempt to use certain drugs to stop the patient's mental abilities from deteriorating further.

But if a drug can make a person with Alzheimer's Disease less likely to loose more mental functioning, what could the same drug to do to a person who has a normal, healthy brain? Could they make him or her even smarter? That's the kind of question brain researchers began to ask about 15 years ago.

Since then several popular books have been published on the subject of brain enhancing drugs and scientific research interest has grown stronger. One such book has predicted that the smart drugs would become a billion dollar business before the decade of the 1990s is over. Furthermore, if new drugs are developed with a proven ability to boost IQ scores and make poor students into straight "A" students, you can be certain that the smart drug business is going to soar into the trillion dollar business category.

How Smart Drugs Work

Today's smart drugs generally work by minimizing damage done to the brain caused by aging or disease. They slow the rate at which the brain decays due to age.

Age is not the only thing which causes the brain to deteriorate. The most common other brain shrinkers are alcohol and drug abuse. The use of tobacco also significantly damages the brain over a long period of time. But other toxins in the environment can have the same effect. For example, if you smell too many automobile fumes, household paint thinners or cleansers, and other common chemicals of every day life, you may suffer brain mass loss as a result.

All of these substances promote what is called oxidation. Oxidation is the same thing as rust. When a piece of metal rusts, it is said to "oxidize." What you probably did not know was that your body, although not made of metal, can "rust" or decay in much the same way metal does. While water an exposure to oxygen causes metal to rust, it is another kind of oxygen that causes your body and brain to rust.

Oxidation rusts your brain by produces substances in the body called free radicals. These are rogue oxygen molecules which are missing one electron. Because they are missing an electron, they will attach themselves to the nearest cell of your body that can fill their empty space. That cell may be a brain cell, for example. This process robs the original cell of its ability to stay in tact, and thus the cell corrupts and dies. In this way, oxidation slowly eats up the brain, and the person who owns that brain progressively loses his or her brain functions and mind.

This is especially harmful to the brain since it is widely believed that brain cells do not regenerate themselves, as do skin cells and, many other kind of cells in the human body. Even though brain cells cannot regenerate, it is possible to deactivate free radicals and repair some of the other damage — including low levels of electric current transmitting chemicals in the brain — and this can be achieved with smart drugs and certain nutrients, such as vitamins. You can stop the brain from rusting, or at least slow the process down.

It is also possible to enhance the brain's natural properties with smart drugs by helping the brain to build new connections. This is a second way that smart drugs can help. Neurons also known as brain cells, are tangled together and interconnected with thousands of other neurons, which all together form what some scientists call the "neural net."

The thicker the neural net, the better your brain functions, and the smarter you will be. most likely. That's because it is easier for one neuron to send information to another neuron. Based on the knowledge we have of current smart drugs, we know it is possible to help the brain to grow a thicker neural net. As these connections are formed when new memories formed, the user can actually learn and memorize things faster and easier. Thicker neurons combined with the right kind of brain chemicals — which we'll talk about more in a minute   for a powerful combination to enhance the brain function, making a person not only smarter, but happier. We'll talk more about happiness in just a bit.

But for now, we just want to make the point that smart drugs can also enhance mental functions by feeding the brain with more oxygen or increasing the levels of neurotransmitting chemicals that carry electric signals from one neuron to another.

Be advised, we are simplifying things a bit here. There's a lot more to the brain than the neural net and the chemicals which ride along on them. But this book is not intended to be a text book for doctors or brain researchers. We want to bring home the exciting developments in brain research to the average person on the street.

Having said that, let's move on further with our discussion of smart drugs.

The great smart drugs debate

It's amazing to know that you can stop your brain from deteriorating with smart drugs and minerals, and even make your brain work more efficiently, but does it mean in actual every day life? Does it mean you can develop a photographic memory? Does it mean you will suddenly find complex subjects, such as quantum mechanics or calculus suddenly easy?

Well, the answer is no. With today's drugs, the changes are not that dramatic. Even though memory, thinking and brain enhancement can be significant in some cases, the reality is often far less significant. On the other hand, many who take smart drugs say that a huge or dramatic change in intelligence, while nice, is not important, because even a 5% increase in your intelligence gives you an edge over the next guy who isn't taking smart drugs. And a small 5% increase in your intelligence is better than no increase. Furthermore, a 5% increase in intelligence can make a 100% difference in your life. For example, in many situation, the person who scores a 90 or above in an employment exam will get hired over the person who scores an 85% or 88%.

People who have tried smart drugs report a wide range of reactions. Some swear the drugs made them smarter and gave them an edge, while others are certain the drugs had no effect on their overall level of intelligence or ability to think. Although the process of how neurochemicals and smart drugs work is known and agreed upon by most scientists, those same scientists have not agreed on whether smart drugs really are effective in younger and healthy people.

A lot of the data we have today on smart drugs comes from tests on animals or from people being treated for or Parkinson's disease and Alzheimer's Disease, two of the most common forms of brain disease in elderly people. But studies with healthy, normal healthy adults have been done as well.. For example, a recent double blind study on late-middle-aged test subjects showed increase in mental functions after four weeks of taking a drug called Piracetam. Studies showing benefits from other drugs in normal test subjects also exist. The same goes for a natural human hormone called pregnenolone. We'll discuss both of these drugs in more detail later in this chapter.

Despite some positive results with the two drugs above and several other drugs tested on healthy people, many researchers and doctors are not at convinced that the data is meaningful,a nd a lot more testing is needed, although just about all admit that the preliminary data tests like these are showing is very exciting and leading scientists in the right direction.

Five Basic Kinds of Smart Drugs
Smart drugs fall into five categories:

1) Synthetic drugs produced by medical chemists in labs, and which, for the most part, are only available by prescription from a licensed medical practitioner.

2) Vitamins. Yes, the ordinary vitamins you eat every day can be considered smart drugs, and we'll discuss why this is so in just a bit.

3) Herbs. Many herbs, such as ginkgo biloba and ginseng have long been considered in folklore to be
intelligence and brain enhancing substances, but it is
only recently that modern science has begun to take
a closer look at these natural substances, and their
amazing power to enhance brain function. You will
find a through discussion of herbs for the brain in
the next chapter.

4) Nutrition. Certain foods can actually enhance and
improve brain function. Foods can easily change
your mood. Indeed, there are "happy" foods and
"sad" foods. For example, have you ever gotten very
depressed after a sugar binge? On the other hand,
have you ever felt light and happy after a meal of
fresh fish, rice and steamed vegetables? No doubt,
many of you have. Foods affect the brain — believe
it. We'll discuss this much more also in the next
chapter.

5) Hormones. These are natural chemicals which your
body manufactures every day, such as estrogen,
testosterone, melatonin and DHEA. But these hormones can also be isolated outside the body and
drugs can be made from them. The most common
example is the drug Premarin, which is estrogen,
most often prescribed to women to cope with
menopause and other problems. Studies now suggest that many of the body's natural hormones can
increase your intelligence level by improving the
health and function of the brain. The prime example
of this is the hormone pregnenolone. We'll have a
thorough discussion of this natural hormone and tell

you how you can possible use it in your life to improve your own mind and brain.

Please keep in mind: whether we're talking about a pill or a slab of fish, what matters are the effects the substance has on the brain, your mood and your intelligence. A food can be a smart drug, just as a food can make you feel more sluggish and mentally blurred — large amounts of sugar and a good example of the latter.

When you know what boosts the brain and what slows it down, you can began your own experimentation including taking some of the prescription drugs we are going to talk about here to enhance your mind and brain. Of course, you need to consult with your medical doctor before you can obtain prescription drugs, and you should also consult with your doctor about any major nutritional changes you also have in the works.

Perhaps your biggest challenge will be finding a doctor who is willing to work with you on this basis. Remember, doctors treat diseases. They are not in the business to make healthy people even better, although there are some specialists that are in the later kind of business.

So let's talk about some of these prescription drugs. As we said, we'll discuss herbs, vitamins and nutrition in greater detail in the next chapter. We'll deal with the prescription drugs right here.

The primary drugs in contention as smart drugs today are:

Smart Drugs

- Piracetam
- Cerebroforte
- Cetam
- Encefalux
- Euvifor
- Genogris
- Nootron
- Normabrain
- Novocetam
- Psycoton
- UCB-6215)

- Avigilen
- Cerebrospan
- Dinagen
- Encetrop
- Gabacet
- Meo-Puren
- Nootropil
- Norzetam
- Pirrozil
- Stimucortex

The most common smart drug on the market today is probably Piracetam. This drug has a wide variety of uses and is very inexpensive. It is used to treat several illnesses, such as alcoholism, dementia and stroke, but also can improve memory and learning in healthy humans. It does that by increasing and improving the flow of information between the right and left hemispheres of the brain, thus helping in creative problem solving. In effect, Piracetam makes the Corpus Callosum more efficient. The Corpus Callosum is is the think tissue filled with nerves that connect right half and left half together. Piracetam is sold as pills and the effective dose is 2400-4800 mg in three divided doses, although some sources recommend significantly smaller dosages ranging from 800 mg to 2400 mg.

The great thing about Piracetam is that it is what is called a "clean drug." That is, it has no known serious side effects, although insomnia, headaches, nausea and stomach disturbances are possible in a very small percentage of people. As with any other smart drugs, a certain amount of experimentation is the best to try and find out the dose that is good for you while keeping in mind the possible toxicity of the drug. Thus, you should never take megadoses, and always go by the rule: a little is better than a lot." Having said this, most researchers agree that Piracetam is very mild and not toxic, which means that you probably can't overdose on it,

But again remember, more is not always better with smart drugs. While a little may improve your mental functioning, a lot may do the opposite — cloud your mind and decrease the efficiency of the way your brain functions.

Piracetam has a synergistic effect with other smart drugs. That means it can work even better to improve your thinking processes if it is combined with one of the following smart drugs: DMAE, centrophenoxine, choline and Hydergine.

Piracetam is a prescription only drug in many countries, including the United States, but is widely available via mail-order from other countries.

Hydergine, also known as:

Circanol, Coristin, D-Ergotox forte, L.U.T., Dacoren, Deapril-ST, Decme, Decril, Defluina, DHE, DHET, dihydroergotoxine, Dulcion, Enirant, Ergodesit, Ergohydrin, ergoloid mesylates, Ergoplus, Insibrin, Nehydrin, Novofluen, Orphol, Perenan, Progeril, Redergin, Simactil, Sponsin, Trigot and Unergol)

Hydergine is another well-known and well understood drug used by many to increase intelligence. It was originally developed to treat senile dementia in elderly people. Hyderfine is said to increase intelligence, memory and recall, and prevent several kinds of brain deterioration. Also, Hydergine is believed to reverse damage done to the brain by free radicals dOne of the most powerful aspects of this drug is its ability to prevent damage to the brain caused by oxygen deprivation. Because of this, emergency room doctors keep it close on hand to treat stoke victims. Administering this drug shortly after a stroke can prevent further, serious brain injury from happening, and can even save the life of the patient.

The best known side-effects of Hydergine are mild nausea, dizziness and headaches. These side effects are very rare, and even though such side-effects have been documented, Hydergine is still considered to be among the cleanest of smart drugs and is also considered to be virtually non-toxic.

The only known danger of Hydergine is when people have abused it by taking very large doses, well beyond the recommended daily dosage. A proper dose of this is anything from 3 mg to 9 mg, although doses as high as 12 mg have been tried on healthy people with no side-effects. You can buy Hydergine tablets in sizes that range from 1 mg to 5 mg per pill. Also, and it is important to note, that Hydergine is most effective when it is divided into three equal doses taken three times a day. Also, side effects, if they occur,may take many months to show up, unless mega-doses are being taken. In the latter case, side effects will quickly present themselves. The legal status of Hydergine is similar to that of Piracetam. You need a doctor's prescription to get it in the United States, but it is available by mail order from other countries.

Vasopressin, also known as:

Diapid, LVP, Lypressin, Postacton, Syntopressin, Adiuretin, SD, DAV Ritter, DDAVP, Desmopressin, Desmospray, Minirin and AVP.

This is another prescription drug, most commonly known as Diapid. This is a trade name for Vasopressin. This drug has long been considered a smart drug by many in the medical community. This drug is actually a brain hormone which you body produces on its own, much like other common hormones, such as melatonin, estrogen or testosterone. It has been used to treat a some kinds of diabetes because it reduces the need to urinate frequently. It has also been used to treat several conditions leading to memory impairment. Vasopressin is taken in the form of a nasal spray - 2 to four sniffs three times a day. Its effects are immediate,a nd you can't mistake them. It almost immediately makes you feel clear headed and increases you ability to focus your mind so that you can grasp new concepts quicker and learn faster. Also, it help yo learn easier.

Vasopressin is most often sold in 12 ml bottles and runs out very quickly if you use it a lot. But using is a lot and often is not a good idea. It can lead to headaches, nose irritation or abdominal cramps. People with diagnosed hypertension or cardiovascular problems should also proceed with caution.

Even though it has some side effects and is not for everyone, this drug, like Peracetam and Hydergine is considered extremely safe. just because this substance is a drug should not make it any worse than many other things that can be just as dangerous — such as coffee and cigarettes. Just as a cup of coffee can cause a person with hypertension to have a stroke or heart attack, a drug like Vasopressin can cause great harm to a person who should not be using it because on an existing condition. Vasopressin is only available as a prescription drug but can be purchased without a doctor's prescription through some foreign markets.

Deprenyl: A Universal Anti-Aging Strategy?

After age 45, the dopamine-containing neurons in the human brain start declining rapidly. It happens to just about everybody. It's aging, and until now, scientists have considered this "normal."

A specific part of the brain called the nigrostriatal region, contains the most dopamine and ages faster than any other part of the brain once dopamine starts disappearing.. People who's brain nigrostriatal regions age prematurely develop symptoms of Parkinson's disease, formerly called the shaking palsy. Age-associated depletion of dopamine also accounts for less noticeable symptoms, like decline in drives, most notably male sex drive.

A One-of-a-Kind Make up for a Smart Drug

Deprenyl provides selective protection against the age-related degeneration of the dopaminergic nervous system. It protects sensitive dopamine-containing neurons from the age-associated increases in glial cells (non-neuron brain cells) and the monoamine oxidase (type B) that they contain. Deprenyl is the first selective inhibitor of MAO-B ever discovered, it is the only one used in clinical practice, and it remains the scientific reference standard for B-type inhibition after more than 40 years.

Deprenyl also competitively inhibits the uptake of dopamine, norepinephrine and epinephrine (collectively referred to as catecholamines) into neurons. This unique ability among the MAO inhibitors prevents the "cheese effect," a dangerous hypertensive reaction caused by neural uptake of tyramine from tyramine-containing foods like aged cheeses, certain wines, yeast, beans, chicken liver and herring. Deprenyl exhibits no significant cheese effect at therapeutic dosages, and only minimal effects at extremely high dosages.

Variable Aging in the Brain

The rate at which dopamine neurons age is apparently quite variable. Prior to age 45, dopamine levels remain fairly stable. Starting at age 45, average dopamine content in healthy individuals decreases linearly 13% per decade. When it reaches approximately 30%, Parkinson symptoms result. Below 10%, death results. Although the average decrease in dopamine is 13% per decade, some individuals exhibit more rapid decline and others less rapid decline. People experiencing rapid dopamine decline manifest with Parkinson's disease. Those with normal or slow decline die before Parkinson symptoms become apparent.

This model of nigrostriatal aging and the development of Parkinson's disease has been advanced by Dr. Jozsef Knoll, the world's most prominent deprenyl researcher. He suggests that Parkinsonism may be a generic condition of the human species that does not currently manifest in very many people because of our limited average lifespan. He also suggests a general strategy of long-term deprenyl use for the prevention of nigrostriatal aging in the above-45-year-old population.

Deprenyl and Antioxidant Defenses

The sensitivity of the dopaminergic nervous system to oxidizing free radicals is well established. Oxidative polymerization of aromatic amino acids (e.g., phenylalanine, tyrosine, dopa, tryptophan) and aromatic monoamine neurotransmitters (e.g., norepinephrine, epinephrine, dopamine and serotonin) lead to the formation of melanin, a black pigment which is a characterizing feature of the nigrostriatal (black-striped) neurons. Chronic deprenyl treatment lessens the rate of melanin production.

Two oxidized derivatives of dopa and dopamine (6-hydroxydopa and 6-hydroxydopamine, respectively) are potent neurotoxins. The protective effect of deprenyl in lessening the neurotoxic effect of these two chemicals appears to correlate with increased antioxidant enzyme levels, superoxide dismutase (SOD) [Knoll, 1989] and catalase. The increase in antioxidant enzymes is proportional to the amount of deprenyl given. The protective influence of deprenyl is selective for dopaminergic neurons; increased SOD is not noted throughout the rest of the brain.

Life Extension and Cognitive Enhancement

Although the long-term use of deprenyl in normal people as a life-extension and cognitive-enhancing drug has yet to be definitively studied, animal research is extensive. Age-associated decrease in sexual performance and hunger drive in rodents (a dopaminergic function) is dramatically inhibited.

The lifespan studies of deprenyl in rodents is equally dramatic all of the control rats die before the first deprenyl-treated rat dies.

The life-extending influence of deprenyl is not mediated through a food-restriction mechanism. Deprenyl-treated animals maintain body weight better than control animals.

Early research with deprenyl in humans (early diagnosed Parkinson patients) shows delayed development of symptoms and delayed need for L-dopa therapy. In combination with other drugs, deprenyl has significantly prolonged the survival of Parkinson patients.

Deprenyl's low level of toxicity, few side-effects, and unique spectrum of pharmacological activities make it ideal for prophylaxis against nigrostriatal aging and the secondary aging symptoms accompanying the decline of the dopaminergic nervous system. Deprenyl is a drug of choice for Parkinson's disease and is currently being established as a treatment for Alzheimer's disease. Eventually, deprenyl may become recognized as a general treatment for aging in the above-45-year-old population.

Centrophenoxine (Lucidril)

Centrophenoxine is a drug that is generally considered to be an anti-aging agent. As least it has worked for lab animals. In studies done on mice and rats, Centrophenoxine increased the lifespan of these animals by one-thirds, or more than 33%. Not only did the rats and mice live longer, they proved themselves smarter than similar rats and mice that did not receive the drug. (That's just what we need — smarter rats!)

Centrophenoxine works by clearing out waste in human cells, including brain cells, or neurons. This waste is called liposfucin. It prevents the normal functioning of neurons when present in too great amounts. When taken (usually as pills) it breaks down to a substance called DMAE in your bloodstream. Researchers believe the final effect of these two drugs ar very similar. A suggested dosage is anything between 1000 and 3000 mg daily, although the dose should be reduced if side effects occur. These side effects are listed as excitability, muscle stiffness or headaches. Pregnant or nursing mothers should not use Centrophenoxine because it has not been determined safe for babies, or fetuses. This drug is not available in the U.S.although its close cousin, DMAE, is widely available from health food stores and pharmacists. In many European counties Centrophenoxine is a prescription drug and DMAE is less common. Now let's talk more about the latter, DMEA.

DMAE (Dimethylaminoethanol)

This drug is also known Deanol-Riker in Europe. It is widely available as a nutritional supplement here in the United States. DMAE works by increasing intelligence, memory, energy levels and learning. It is also said to extends life span and make a person feel more "happy."

Better yet, all these benefits are felt by the individual within a half-hour of swallowing this drug, most often taken as a liquid. The effect wears off after a few hours.

Some people have reported a build up of tolerance to DMAE after several weeks of use. If tolerance builds up it can be handled by discontinuing the use for a few weeks. Adverse contraindications are rare, but minor side effects include muscle tension or hypertension. Overdosing may cause insomnia or dull-headedness, so it is better to start with a low dose first. A suggested dose is from 300 mg up to 1000 mg daily in two divided doses usually morning and afternoon).

Determining the correct dose is not difficult: simply start with a low enough dose and gradually build up until you notice no further benefits, although this method could be tricky. That's because many feelings, such as happiness, are highly psychological and subjective. Also, it's important to note that DMAE may cause just the opposite of the desired effect! That is, it may make you feel dumb and sluggish if you take too much. So there is a point of diminishing returns with this drug. Overdosing is not recommended. One common misconception about DMAE is that its like caffeine, but it is not. It's even safer than caffeine in small doses.

Also, DMAE does not cause nervousness nor depression, as coffee can, and is a much safer and better general purpose stimulant than coffee.

Smart nutrients

Antioxidants

There are several vitamins that are classified as antioxidants, namely vitamin E, C and A (beta-carotene). Reported benefits from antioxidants are anti-aging effects and protection from damage to brain cells. Recommended dosages vary greatly, but here's general dosage suggestion: water soluble vitamin E (100-500 IU daily), Vitamin C (200-500 mg daily) and beta-carotene (25 000 - 30 000 IU daily). Note that Vitamin A is toxic even if not lethal when overdosed, so taking beta-carotene (which your body turns into vitamin A) instead is recommended. Pregnant women should not supplement with vitamin A (nor beta-carotene) unless prescribed by a doctor. All of these should be readily available at your local pharmacist.

• B vitamins

There are twelve different B vitamins, of which four have been shown to have positive effects on the nervous system. Thiamine (vitamin B1) is also considered an antioxidant and the recommended dosage is between 25 and 150 mg daily although some sources report doses as high as 1 000 mg.

Niacin (B3) helps to improve memory and to combat stress. Recommended dosage is 100-200 mg daily taken with an antacid (e.g. bicarbonate of soda). Doses exceeding 50 mg may first cause flushing i.e. a feeling of blood rushing to the head. Some people have also reported itching as a side-effect. These effects should go away after continued use.

Pyridoxine (B6) promotes the manufacture of neurotransmitters in your brain, and as such, is vital for your brain to function properly. In some careful studies, B6 was shown to increase life-span and to decrease stress. Recommended dosage is 50-100 mg daily. Doses over 125 mg can be neurotoxic over longer periods of time and should be avoided. B6 is the only vitamin of these four B vitamins that has been know to be toxic.

Cyanocobalamin (B12) is useful when fighting fatigue as it helps the release of energy from food. It has also been show to increase learning in laboratory animals. A daily amount of 100-200 mcg is suggested along with 400 mcg of folic acid. All of these vitamins are best taken as a B-complex, so that supplementing one type of vitamin B will not cause a deficiency of another type. Available at any drug store, department store or supermarket.

• Choline and Lecithin

Lecithin and choline are precursors of acetylcholine (they are turned into acetylcholine in your body) which transmits electric impulses in your brain. They have been show to improve short term memory in normal humans. Both of the nutrients offer basically the same benefits, although you can get away with taking smaller amounts of choline as all of lecithin is not transformed into acetylcholine.

Suggested intake is 3 grams of choline four times a day (that means 12 grams/day) and a bit more for lecithin in two doses. Both should be taken with a large amounts of B5 (c. 1 gram per dose) to help the conversion to acetylcholine. Choline can cause a fishy odor (which is not dangerous, unless you're in a crucial part of your relationship) that can be avoided by eating yogurt. In large doses it can also cause diarrhea, which is a sure sign to cut down the dosage. Both can be bought at health food stores as liquid or as capsules. Both should be stored in your refrigerator in an airtight container.

• **Amino acids**

Although the use of amino acids are usually attributed to body builders, some of the aminos are generally known as smart nutrients also. They are essential in building neuro-transmitters in your brain and low levels of amino acids in one's diet can result in tiredness and lack of concentration. Supplementing them should be considered especially if one is a vegetarian on a low fat diet (low fat diet is sometimes missing in proteins). Phenylalanine is the most common of brain boosting amino acids; it will help one to fight off stress and it may also elevate one's mood and increase alertness. A compound called DL-phenylalanine taken daily at the dose of 1 000 to 1 500 mg should be enough, followed by 50mg of vitamin B5 and half a gram of vitamin C. Phenylalanine is best taken on an empty stomach, because it competes with proteins to cross the blood brain barrier.

A word of warning: if you're psychotic or taking MAO-inhibitor drugs (such as Deprenyl) you should not use phenylalanine because phenylalanine competes with tryp-tophan (a protein) in crossing the blood brain barrier these substances should not be taken together. If phenylalanine prevents tryptophan from crossing the blood brain barrier, then you may end up with lower serotonin levels, which in severe cases can lead to depression and aggressiveness. Foods rich in L-tryptophan include: Cottage cheese, milk, meat, fish, turkey, bananas, dried dates, peanuts or gener-ally all foods rich in protein. Again, avoid taking phenylala-nine with these foods, and you will get better results if you take it on an empty stomach.

There are also several other amino acids, such as Glutamine, Arginine, Tryptophan and Taurine, but as the safety and usefulness of all these have not been settled. In the early 90's there was a nasty case of contaminated tryptophan supplement resulting in the death of several people, causing FDA to ban tryptophan supplements. This does not mean that tryptophan cannot be safe, it's just that currently it's not available as a supplement in USA and most other countries (at least not without a prescription). Only future research will show their ability as safe nootropics and until then it is wiser to settle for other types of supplements. There's plenty to choose from after all.

• Herbs

Herbs are probably the most controversial brain boosters in the sense that they have little scientific backup for their claimed effects. Although people in the medical profession may not deny the power of herbs altogether they usually will not recommend them unless the active ingredient in the herb is known along with its effects. This is only applies to western medicine, as herbs are widely accepted and used in the traditional medical craft of China. As long as western medicine will scorn herbs as a just another snake oil, people using them will use folk wisdom in choosing the right ingredients for their mix. Mixing of herbs is considered essential as herbalists claim that many herbs have little effect on their own, but combined they're supposedly very potent. For us busy westerners unable to pick our own herbs two forms of preserved herb essences remain, mainly freeze-dried and alcohol based extracts.

These two preserving methods are supposed to retain the power of the herbs for long periods.

Here's a sampling of some of the most well known brain boosting herbs.

• **Ginkgo Biloba**

The leaf extract from the oldest tree on earth, Ginkgo Biloba is a widely used brain booster. It increases blood circulation in the tiny blood vessels of the brain and effects usually attributed to it include improved memory, reasoning and alertness. Ginkgo extract is also accepted by the medical community in Europe and it is widely prescribed by doctors. In addition to its other properties ginkgo is also an antioxidant and it helps your brain to build its own fuel called ATP. It comes usually in the form of liquid, although powder is also available and should be preferred. The suggested dosage is 120-160 mg of ginkgo extract that contains 24% active ingredients ginkgo flavonoids.

The extract should be taken in three divided doses as ginkgo leaves the body within six hours of ingestion. Extracts are available from health food stores almost everywhere, but the potency may not be that great. The ingredient to keep an eye on when choosing ginkgo products is ginkgo flavonoids or ginkgo heterosides. The more extract has this the better it is. If only low potency extracts are available one should up the dosage even up to 1000 mg. There are no reported side-effects in the medical literature, but some users have complained about stomach troubles at high doses. Effects are usually noticeable after two or three weeks of continued use, although sometimes it may take as long as two months.

• Ginseng

Chinese medicine has used ginseng root successfully for 4000 years and during that time it has had several medical uses. Ginseng has been used to treat fatigue, abnormal blood pressure and quite oddly even insomnia and cancer. It is generally thought of as an all around medicine that has no specific use, so people use it to get various different results. Stress and fatigue relief are among the most commonly give reasons for taking ginseng extract. It works by regulating the blood sugar levels and heart beat, increasing blood flow and metabolism - to name just a few.

It is often referred to as the 'wonder drug' due to its multitude of uses. As ginseng has a long tradition of use it is available in several different forms, such as powder, pastes, tablets, ginseng tea and the root itself. Tea and extracts are the best forms, because the active ingredients gets into your blood faster from these forms. Both products have a distinct bitter taste as does the root itself. If you plan to use the root, you're better of chewing than swallowing it, because ginseng is very hard to digest.

Dosage is anything from 500 to 4000 mg daily in divided doses according to Smart Drugs and Nutrients. When buying one should look for Korean or Siberian ginseng as these are usually thought to be most potent, whereas American ginseng is least potent. One should start noticing effects after two months of continuous use, although ginseng may have much faster short term effects as well. People with high blood pressure should start at the lower end of the dose spectrum.

• Gotu-kola

Another extremely interesting plant from the east is called gotu-kola. This is a plant that has been used to improve wound healing and to treat many kinds of skin conditions. Gotu-kola is also believed to positively affect brain functioning by reducing nervousness, stress, and anxiety. Gotu-kola has a mild tranquilizing effect on those who take it. Unfortunately, few credible scientific studies on this plant exist (unlike ginseng and ginkgo biloba, which are both well researched), but at least one study shows it to improve concentration. It can be bought from health food stores in various forms and a dose of two leaves a day — and chew them but do not swallowed them — to get the best desired effect. Finally, a plant very similar to gotu-kola in its effects and use is called fo-ti-tieng, which can be used in place of gotu-kola.

• Caffeine

Yes, it is one of the most common and oldest stimulants known to humankind, but caffeine, as we have said elsewhere, can truly be considered a smart drug — with certain drawbacks and some negative long-term consequences which may actually make it a kind of "dumb drug." Of course, we know that caffeine is named by many people to be the only thing that can jump start them in the morning. Because of this, caffeine is generally considered to improve mental performance, and thus intelligence. But as we all know, caffeine also makes people anxious and irritable if used enough and often enough. Caffeine is also very addictive, especially when combined with sugar, as it very often is. Caffeine is also an effective diuretic, meaning is causes people to urinate more often. In fact, when you drink coffee or soft drinks that contain caffeine, you are actually causing your body to have a net loss of water. And one of the worst things for the brain is not having enough water to run on. Not only does caffeine dehydrate your body, it also causes the human body to pass out many other vital minerals and vitamins, especially those of the B family. As we talked about earlier, B vitamins are vital links to a healthy brain, and increases intelligence. More going to the bathroom means more depletion of everything in your body. So once again, we see caffeine as a fine stimulant, but the long-term effect is the opposite. It can even make you more sluggish and tired in the long run because it robs your body and brain of vital nutrients.

If we leave the performance claims aside, the main source of caffeine for most people is coffee. Coffee has been proven to hinder digestion, and raise cholesterol levels. It also may cause severe withdrawal symptoms such as migraine headaches when you try to quit.Heavy users can find themselves in a condition not all too different from major anxiety neurosis.

Furthermore, caffeine has still another action on the brain. Caffeine causes the blood vessels of the brain to constrict, or grow smaller. This is why caffeine is added to many common headache remedies. Most headaches are caused by blood vessels in the brain which expand, or dilate, putting pressure on the brain and this causing pain. Caffeine shrinks them back down, getting rid of the pressure and usually the headache — but this also obviously means that less blood is flowing to the brain. Less blood to the brain means less oxygen and less glucose, or sugar. So while the short-term effect of caffeine is to wake you up and give you a jumpstart, the long-term effect is that is actually robs the brain of vital oxygen and sugar, making you dumber, not smarter.

So what's the answer? Should you use caffeine, or stay away from it? Most researchers agree that a little caffeine is an excellent idea, and a lot is not a good idea. A cup or two in the morning will give you a boost, but then you should rely on more constructive brain boosting techniques and foods — many of which you have read about in other parts of this book — to get you through the rest of the day.

Finally, think of caffeine as a drug, because it certainly is a drug. Unfortunately, our society considers caffeine to mostly to be a food additive. It's not only in coffee and soft drinks, but in many other foods, especially chocolates and other candies. You see, caffeine is also a flavor enhancer, and food chemists know that. They also know it is mildly addictive. So putting caffeine in, say, Diet Coke, not only has the effect of making Diet Coke taste better, it also makes it addictive, causing people to use more, and more importantly, buy more. Believe it, the folks at the Coca-Cola bottling company wold not mind it if their product was not only good tasting, but addictive as well. That can only be good for the bottom line. And as we said, caffeine seems to be many times more addictive when combined with sugar, or other sweeteners. So once you start the candy and soft drink habit, cutting back may be extremely difficult. Not as difficult as say, cigarettes or chewing tobacco, yet difficult enough to cause some misery in your life.

Research on caffeine's benefits is divided: some claim it improves performance while others proclaim it actually decreases performance. What is for sure is that several million people swear by it daily.

So be wary with caffeine. A little is a brain booster, but a lot can have too many overriding medical side effects to make it worthwhile.

Obtaining Smart Drugs from Other Countries by Mail Order

Depending on what country you live in, the availability of all of the drugs we have told you about may or may not be available. In some countries, you can simply buy many of these drugs off the shelf of any drug store. In others, they are available only by prescription. And some are not available at all, except on the "black market."

It is usually best to go and ask at your local pharmacy first. You may get lucky and find everything you need. If the local drug store cannot help you out, you can try mail order - that is, buy these drugs in a different country and have them shipped to you via mail or private carrier, such as Federal Express.

Mail order, in fact, is the most common way that people buy smart drugs if the they are unavailable over-the-counter in their own country of residence. Additionally, there are a vast multitude of places that people can order drugs. Unfortunately, there is often a few glitches to overcome in many cases. For example, and depending on your country's laws on the drugs in question, you may or may not be able to import the drugs from their country of origin. FIn the United States smart drug shipments have been often been seized by the Federal Drug Administration (FDA) during the past several years. The FDA has also gone further by putting many companies under surveillance, including the most common smart drug suppliers. Thus, all shipments from those companies will be seized by customs officials at the U.S. border. To add insult to injury, after your smart drugs are confiscated, you may lose the money you paid for them because the FDA has no legal obligation to repay you, nor does the supplier. In some cases, people have been successful in getting the FDA to return the package to the sender, who will then refund your money, if they are so inclined. The problem is, however, by that time, you may have spent more in time and resources than you would have originally paid for the smart drugs in the first place.

If the package is returned some suppliers are willing to refund you or try sending the package to an alternative address.

If you are lucky enough to live in Europe, Canada, Australia or practically anywhere else besides the United States, it is quite possible to order smart drugs via mail order. The usual procedure is to send a money order or a personal check to the company you are ordering from along with the order. Most order take a month or two to process and you can get your order from your local post office or - in the best case scenario - from your doorstep. It is a good idea to check the law on importing prescription drugs for personal use before ordering, even though it has become quite common such things as experimental drugs for the treatment of AIDS to move through the mail.

If you nevertheless want to find out what is available, you can obtain a price and product list of all smart drugs available from overseas venues. Most will be glad to send you a list for free, although sending an international reply coupon (IRC) along with your query will not hurt your case. You can get IRCs from any post office).

Once you find out what is available, you can proceed to figure out a way to get the drugs into your hands. Many people take personal trips to the country of smart drug origin, buy their drugs and then simply return home with the products in their suitcase. In most instances, these drugs are not confiscated. Generally, port officials agree that anything that you can buy legally off the shelf in another country can be brought back by the people who buy them. This is only true, however, if the drugs are bought in small amounts. Few customs officials will get alarmed by a bottle or two of what looks like prescription drugs or vitamins, but someone who tries to clear a large suitcase stuffed with pills is likely to find trouble.

NOTES:

_____

_____

_____

_____

_____

_____

_____

_____

_____

_____

_____

_____

_____

Chapter 7
The Brain Hormone

A lot of people have trouble with memory, and not just the elderly. Many people when they turn 40 notice a remarkable drop off in their ability to recall simple facts from day to day, from moment to moment. Some say it is only "natural" to lose some memory power as you advance in years. Some even consider it a kind of sweet aspect of getting old. We all know an elderly grandfather or grandmother who had trouble with small fact or big facts and have either said, oh well, or that's kind of cute.

But just ask them to see if it's an "oh well" situation. They'll tell you "No! "I want a better memory back," they'll say. "I want my youth back!" The fact is, losing your memory is never a good thing! It's scary , frustrating and definitely not natural!

Loss of memory is a disease in the strongest sense of the word. It is a condition that robs you of your quality of life. It impairs your ability to work at jobs that require mental acuity and alertness. Radical memory loss effects about 10 percent of all people over the age of 65, Although about 20 percent of these cases may be due to treatable causes such as toxic drug reactions, and such.

One of the keys to stopping memory loss from happening to an aging brain is the hormone pregnenolone. Many scientists consider this hormone the true key to maintaining a healthy mind late into life. This hormone seems to not only aid the proper functioning of the memory, but many of the critical aspects of the mind, even our mental feelings of happiness and well-being.

So what is pregnenolone? This hormone comes from the substance we all know as cholesterol. Of course, we've all come to think that cholesterol is a bad thing. That's not hard to understand considering all the attention doctors give about the dangers of high cholesterol levels, and the many health problems it causes for the human body.

But it's important to acknowledge the fact that cholesterol is not all bad. There is "good" cholesterol and "bad" cholesterol. Medical researchers, however, now think that there really is no such thing as bad cholesterol, only too much of a good thing. Truly, life itself would be impossible without cholesterol. Additionally, researchers have now concluded that too little cholesterol in the blood can lead to a whole host of other kinds of diseases, including mental illness. A recent and significant study showed that a large percentage of prisoners had low cholesterol levels. Apparently, too little cholesterol in the blood is a major factor in anti-social behavior, including violent anger and moderate to severe depression.

Cholesterol is needed by the body to produce vitamin D, which is a vital part of many physical functions, including the body's ability to absorb calcium. Vitamin D also aides in the manufacturing of myelin, the sheath of material that coats the nerves. Those people who suffer from degenerative diseases such as multiple sclerosis are unable to produce myelin, and also have their existing myelin erode from its position on the nerves. The result is a loss of muscle control, and life-time of crippling weakness, and loss of use of the most fundamental bodily movements.

The human body breaks down cholesterol into the hormone pregnenolone and other hormones, including DHEA. Pregnenolone is sometimes called the "mother hormone" because other hormones such as DHEA and estrogen and testosterone come from it.

Pregnenolone is manufactured in the brain and by the adrenal cortex, glands positioned on top of the kidneys. The two parts of the gland, the inner portion, or medulla, and the outer portion, or cortex, are like separate endocrine organs. They are composed of different types of tissue and perform different functions. The adrenal medulla, composed of chromaffin, secretes the hormone epinephrine, also called adrenaline, in response to stimulation of the sympathetic nervous system at times of stress. The medulla also secretes the hormone norepinephrine, which plays a role in maintaining normal blood circulation. The hormones of the medulla are called catecholamines. Unlike the cortex, the medulla can be removed without endangering the life of an individual.

The adrenal outer layer, or cortex, secretes about 30 steroid hormones, but only a few are secreted in significant amounts. Aldosterone, one of the most important hormones, regulates the salt and water balance in the body. Cortisone and hydrocortisone are also vital; they regulate fat, carbohydrate, and protein metabolism. Also secreted are adrenal sex steroids, which have a minor influence on the reproductive system. Modified glucocorticoids, now produced synthetically, are superior to naturally secreted steroids for treatment of Addison's disease and other disorders.

Like many other hormones in the human body, pregnenolone production drops off in the human body as it ages. By the time most people hit age 75, their bodies are producing about 60 percent less of the hormone as it was at age 30. This is significant because, as we said, pregnenolone is the "parent" to other vital hormones in the body. Lose your pregnenolone and you lose a lot of other vital, brain enhancing hormones.

Pregnenolone and Memory

Before we look at how pregnenolone aides the memory, let's take a closer loot at what memory is.

Surprisingly, scientists actually do not yet understand many things about human memory and many of the ideas and theories about it are still quite controversial. For example, most scientists agree that it is very useful to describe human memory as a set of STORES which are "places" to put information, plus a set of PROCESSES that that act on the stores.

A very simple model might contain 3 different stores:

- The Sensory Information Store (SIS)
- The Short-Term Store (STS)
- The Long-Term Store (LTS)

... and 3 processes

- Encoding (putting information into a store)
- Maintenance (keeping it "alive")
- Retrieval (finding encoded information)

A theory of human memory should not only identify a set of processes and stores, but also be able to help answer questions such how long it will take to retrieve accessible information and when information will be forgotten (become inaccessible). To do this, the theory must specify properties of the processes and stores. For example, a store might have a "maximum capacity" — in other words, a maximum quantity of information that it can hold at a given time. If we know a store's capacity and what happens when that capacity is exceeded, we will be able to predict that certain information will be forgotten at certain times.

In the relatively simple model of memory presented here, sensory information enters the Sensory Information Store (SIS) and is either ignored or paid attention to. Ignored information doesn't last very long. New perceptual information quickly writes over (masks) the old, a process sometimes described as "interference." Attended information is not only protected from interference, it is processed by higher-level mechanisms that figure out what it means. For instance, information in the SIS might indicate a bright red object somewhere ahead. Attending to this information might reveal that there it is a stop-sign. Once information is processed in this way, it can be encoded into the short-term store (STS).

Usually, the STS is described as having a limited storage capacity (seven, plus or minus two items) that "decay" and become inaccessible after a relatively brief interval (estimates range from 12 to 30 seconds). In addition to decay, loss of information from the STS can occur by interference when new information displaces older information. Interference does not always cause information to be lost, but may instead produce memory retrieval errors in which one recalls information that is similar to but not identical with that which is needed.

Information can be maintained in STM for relatively long periods using maintenance rehearsal (MR), a term describing the act of mentally repeating the information to be maintained. In many cases, the reason one wishes to maintain information in the STS is to allow time for it to be encoded into the long-term store (LTS), and thus become more permanently available.

However, maintenance rehearsal does not appear to be very efficient way to get the memory into long-term memory. Another memory maintenance technique, elaboration rehearsal (ER) seems to work better.

Long-term memory can store a very large quantity of information and can maintain that information for very long periods of time. It holds many different kinds of information including: facts, events, motor and perceptual skills, knowledge of physical laws, spatial models of familiar environments, attitudes and beliefs about ourselves and others, etc. Many different factors seem to affect the difficulty of accessing a memory in the LTS. These factors include: the similarity between current conditions and those that existed when the memory was stored, how recently the memory was last used, its degree of inter-relatedness to other knowledge, its uniqueness relative to other LTS information, and so on. Much scientific research remains to be done to specify the effects of these factors in detail and to determine the mechanisms by which they produce their effects.

In general, memories are less clear and detailed than perceptions, but occasionally a remembered image is complete in every detail. This phenomenon, known as eidetic imagery, is usually found in children, who sometimes project the image so completely that they can spell out an entire page of writing in an unfamiliar language that they have seen for a short time.

To date, many drugs have been developed to aid memory in those people who are having trouble with it. Unfortunately, not all of these drugs are effective and they may have negative side effects.

But new research indicates that the very best memory drugs may be the natural hormone pregnenolone. Extensive studies have already been performed on mice in a laboratory setting. Mice who were taught specific tasks, such as finding their way through mazes, choosing specific doors, etc. learned to perform these tasks with spectacular more efficiency when give injections of pregnenolone. They also could remember their tasks weeks later with far better clarity than those who did not receive pregnenolone injections.

Can it work the same miracles on human memory? As it turns out, pregnenolone's effect on the improvement of memory has been understood by medical researchers for more than 50 years! In studies done at the University of Massachusetts tested subjects on specific memory tasks and found that pregnenolone vastly improved the performance of human memory in a variety of laboratory testing situations. Pregnenolone was also given to people in the "real world" including pilots and factory workers, and again, those who took the hormone showed definite improvement in how they were able to perform their jobs. Not only were they able to perform their work better, they also reported feeling less stress, and a generally greater sense of joy and satisfaction with how they felt about their work and lives.

It is unknown why after such positive results science did not look further into pregnenolone as a memory enhancer. Most likely, there was a lot of general concern about side effects and a lot of unknowns since knowledge of the body's chemistry was far less advanced than it is today. One negative side-effect, for example, was an increased feeling of stress and anxiety on behalf of some of the subjects. This makes sense because pregnenolone boosts the body's production of corticosteroids, the primary stress causing hormones.

Today, scientists are taking a closer look at pregnenolone and its effect on not only memory, but a variety of human thought processes.

At the St. Louis University School of Medicine, doctors administered pregnenolone and a placebo to two group of older men and women. Three hours after taking the hormone, they were asked to perform a battery of standard memory tests, and other tests involving use of the critical thinking factors of the brain. Those given pregnenolone showed improvement, but not improvement across the board. Amazingly, the differences varied by sex. Men tended to work visual spatial tasks better and women improved in their verbal recall skills. As we will later see, the reason for the difference between male and female reaction to pregnenolone probably has a lot to do with the fact that testosterone, the male hormone, and estrogen, the female hormone, are derived from pregnenolone. Thus. men who receive pregnenolone supplements probably favor using is as eventual testosterone while women favor it as an estrogen derivative.

Depression

Perhaps America's No. 1 disease, depression afflicts as many as 20 of every 100 people. Many of these people suffer from a number of different but significant depressive symptoms at any one time. Also, more than 30 percent percent of all people can expect to suffer from at least some kind of depression over the course of a lifetime. The disorder strikes men and women of all ages, in all segments of society, but most studies indicate that women are more prone to depression than men.

Depression is characterized by feelings of worthlessness, guilt, sadness, helplessness, and hopelessness. In contrast to normal sadness or the grief accompanying the loss of a loved one, clinical depression is persistent and severe. It is accompanied by a variety of related symptoms, including disturbances in sleep and eating, loss of initiative, self-punishment, withdrawal and inactivity, and loss of pleasure. Psychologists divide depression into two major categories. In both, the predominant symptom is a disturbance in mood. One form of the disorder, depressive disorder, is marked only by episodes of depression. The other, bipolar or manic depressive illness, is characterized by alternating depressed and manic episodes.

In major depression or the depressed phase of bipolar illness, a depressed mood predominates, although the patient may not be aware of feeling sad. Typically, he or she loses all interest in and withdraws from usual activities. Symptoms include sleep disturbances, loss of appetite or greatly increased appetite, inability to concentrate or to make decisions, slowed thinking and decreased energy, feelings of worthlessness, guilt, hopelessness, and helplessness, diminished sexual interest; and recurrent thoughts of suicide and death, sometimes leading to actual suicide.

In the manic phase of bipolar illness, the patient's mood can be elevated, expansive, or irritable. Behavior is bizarre and sometimes obnoxious. Other symptoms include excessive talkativeness, racing thoughts, and grandiose ideas; greatly increased social, sexual, and work activity; distractibility; loss of judgment; and a decreased need for sleep.

Both depressive and bipolar disorders run in families. Almost certainly a predisposition to these disorders is genetically transmitted. Thus, the risk of a depressive disorder is greater in the families of depressive patients than in the population at large. The higher proportion of depression in women may be biologically induced, or it may be that women learn social roles that favor feelings of helplessness. Because women in trouble are more likely to seek help than men, statistics reporting a higher incidence of depression among women than among men may be explained, at least in part, by an underdiagnosis of depression in men.

Studies have suggested that genetic predisposition to depression may be linked with an abnormal sensitivity to the neurotransmitter acetylcholine . Receptors for acetylcholine have been found to occur in excessive numbers in the skin of a number of patients suffering from depressive disorders.

Fortunately, depressive disorders are considered among the most treatable in psychiatry. The usual treatment in modern practice involves administration of a drug plus supportive psychotherapy. Two major classes of drugs are used to treat depressive disorders: the tricyclic/tetracyclic antidepressants and the monoamine oxidase inhibitors.

The latter require following a special diet because they interact with tryamine, which is found in cheeses, beer, wine, chicken livers, and other foods, and causes elevation of blood pressure. The tricyclic antidepressants require no special diet; common generic drugs in this class are amitriptyline, desipramine, doxepin, and imipramine. Lithium carbonate, a common mineral, is used to control the manic phase of manic-depressive illness. In smaller doses, it is also used to regulate the mood fluctuations of this bipolar disorder.

Today, the medical community, with some strong who disagree, considers the drug most commonly called Prozac to be a true revolution in the treatment of depression.

Prozac is actually one of many drugs classified as serotonin reuptake inhibitors.

As this classification indicates, Prozac and its sister drugs inhibit the flow of a substance called serotonin in the brain. Medical researchers have recently found that shortly after ingestion, foods influence the release of important brain chemicals and that carbohydrate foods, in particular, trigger the release of serotonin, which, in turn, suppresses the desire for carbohydrates. Such a mechanism may have evolved to prevent people from glutting themselves on carbohydrates and failing to procure harder-to-find protein. Until recent times, carbohydrate foods were far more accessible than protein. Serotonin is believed to work in complex relationships with insulin and several amino acids, especially tryptophan, all of which participate in monitoring the appetite for various food types. In this same area of research, nutrition experts are trying to unravel the relationship between diabetes and obesity and the role that sweets play for people with these afflictions.

Serotonin is found in many neurons in the brain stem; collectively, these neurons form so-called serotoninergic pathways. Noradrenaline is found in other nerve cells, and together they make up noradrenergic pathways. Similarly, nerve cells containing acetylcholine make up cholinergic pathways. Recent research indicates that the regulation of body temperature, eating behavior, and perhaps sleep depends significantly on a fine balance in the activity of these chemically coded pathways.

Depression may be caused by some sort of malfunction in the production, breakdown, and cellular activity of the neurotransmitters in the limbic system. A fundamental action on the brain of a tranquilizer or other mind-altering drug is to restore the balance between two or more neuro-transmitters or to otherwise alter a certain neurotransmitter system. Amino acids and hormone-like substances found in brain cellsófor example, peptidesóalso are believed to play an important role in moderating the activity of nerve cells and the transmission of their impulses.

Thousands of neuroscientists throughout the world are today involved in studying these chemical systems. Human understanding of how the brain operates, from its basic physiology to its role in learning and emotion, lies in gaining knowledge of the brain's chemistry under normal and abnormal conditions.

Serotonin reuptake inhibitors are still at the forefront of the battle against depression, but at last, its star is beginning to tarnish. For one reason, European doctors have discovered that a common herb known as St. John's Wort, is perhaps far more effective at treating depression than the super high tech and super synthetic Prozac and its cousins.

St. John's Wort (wort is the old English word for flower) is a common name for annual and perennial herbs and shrubs of the family Clusiaceae, native to subtropical and temperate regions worldwide. Some species of the wide-spread genus Hypericum are cultivated in garden borders and rock gardens. The plants have opposite, toothless leaves, generally dotted with blackish spots, which are oil-bearing glands.

Heretofore considered a pesky weed which American farmers have tried to eliminate, this plant may revolutionize the treatment of depression. It has already nearly drive

Prozac out of the market in Germany and a couple of other European nations.

And what about pregnenolone? With Prozac and St. John's Wort already carrying on a fierce battle against the dragon of depression, does pregnenolone have anything new to offer. The answer is yes. That's because the "miracles" of Prozac and St. John's Wort are not miracles for everyone. There is a significant segment of the population that does not respond to either of the above, so there is always room for "one more" depression treatment regime.

Pregnenolone may be the perfect "gap filler" in the modern arsenal of depression medications.

Furthermore, the decline in the natural hormone levels of the body almost invariably coincide with a certain loss of zest or interest in the daily activities of life.

In a recent study, researchers discovered that elderly people who are depressed have lower levels of pregnenolone in their cerebral spinal fluid, a fluid which engulfs the brain. Also depressed people seem to contain too much of a neurotransmitter called GABA. The function of GABA is to protect the brain from getting overheated, an important function to be sure. Problems arise, however, when the brain gets too much of a good thing.

In the case of too much GABA, the brain becomes sluggish, and neurotransmitter flow is inhibited to a degree. Pregnenolone appears to counter the thickening of GABA, and hence, may be a treatment for depression, or a general feeling of low energy and lack of ambition or zest for life. Studies still need to be done. Pregnenolone's effect on depression is still waiting for large-scale tests to prove out the theory of its counter-effect on depression.

Conclusions:

We offer you this information on the hormone pregnenolone as yet another alternative to improve you mind among the many other suggests we have given you throughout this book.

You will be glad to know that you can easily buy pregnenolone in any health food store, however we do strongly suggest that you consult with your doctor before you begin adding this supplement to your daily routine.

NOTES:

_____

_____

_____

_____

_____

_____

_____

_____

_____

_____

_____

_____

_____

_____

Chapter 8
Simple Brain Exercises That Build Mental Power

You can build up your biceps by lifting weights. You can flatten your stomach by doing daily sets of sit-ups. You can beef up your legs muscles by jogging a mile or two every day.

But what about your brain? Unlike your arms or legs, the brain is not a movable part. Therefore, it would seem only common sense that there is no true physical exercise one can perform to increase the fitness and power of the brain.

But this is wrong.

The fact is, there are many exercises you can perform every day that will make your brain more fit, make it function more efficiently, make you smarter, more clear headed, and make you feel all around terrific.

A healthy, fine-tuned, well-exercised brain means everything about your life is improved. Better memory. More

---

creative ideas. Better more restful sleep. Happier, brighter moods more often — in fact — most of the time. Little or no depression and fewer "blues."

Just as the right foods, the right attitude and working in snyc with your brain rhythms will improve your overall brain function, adding exercise is like a cherry on the top. It rounds out a total brain program that super charges your well being and puts you on the road to happiness for good!

Rejuvenating the Midbrain

What exactly is the midbrain, and why is it so important?

We've already talked about the different parts of the brain elsewhere in this book, but just a brief review here will help you understand why certain kinds of exercise can have a strong influence on the brain, in particular, the midbrain.

When you look at it from the outside, the brain has three distinct parts, all of which are connected. They are:

1) The cerebrum

2) The cerebellum

3) The brain stem.

The brain stem most often refers to all the structures that are between the cerebrum and the spinal cord.

These include: the diencephalon, the midbrain, the pons, and something called the medulla. Don't worry! We're not going to quiz you on all of this!

Anyway, all of the above arise from the embryonic fore-brain and midbrain, and the midbrain is what we are inter-ested in this chapter. Note that there are more parts to the brain than what we have mentioned here, including three membranes called meninges. The outer one, the dura mater, is tough and shiny. The middle membrane, the arachnoid layer, encloses the brain loosely and does not slip down into the brain's many ridges. The inner mem-brane, the pia mater, consists mainly of small blood vessels that adhere to the surface of the brain.

The Midbrain has three parts

Just as the whole brain is divided into three parts, the midbrain, also called the "mesencephalon" is also divided into three parts.

The first consists of the cerebral peduncles. These are fiber systems that conduct impulses to and from the cere-brum.

The second is the corpora quadrigemina, which are four bodies that relay signals through the sight and sound path-ways.

The third is a central canal, which scientists call the aqueduct of Sylvius. Around this thing is gray matter that has been associated with the way we feel pain and may have a lot to do with addictive behavior, which does not concern us here.

It interesting to note that all animals with a backbone — from fish to humans — have a brain composed of the same three basic subdivisions found in the human brain: hindbrain, midbrain, and forebrain.

What that tells us is that the midbrain is extremely integral to our entire existence. When we seek to improve our brain, rejuvenating the midbrain is essential. As we explained above, everything between the cerebrum — the higher brain — must pass through the midbrain before it gets to the spinal cord and out to the rest of your body.

A healthy midbrain is kind of what total brain health pivots around. Also, as we mentioned, how you see (sight) and how your hear (sound) is relayed through the structures of the midbrain.

When you were a baby, as you crawled across the floor, as you looked up above your bed and observed the faces that looked down at you, the toys hanging above your crib — they all helped develop the way your brain handled sights. Also, your midbrain needed to learn how to process sounds in your infant years. Sight and sounds are almost always connected. When a big face leaned over your crib, it usually made a strange sound that you soon learned was something called "talking." Eventually, you realized that people made sound when they moved their mouths and that seeing and hearing were somehow connected.

Later, when you started crawling around, you needed to build a relationship between what your hands were grasping for and what you were seeing. Sound helped orient you in your world.

Health care researchers now believe that adults can still benefit from doing all these things that we once did as infants! In fact, studies show that actually getting down on our hands and knees and crawling around on the floor can have a tremendous, stimulating effect on the midbrain, and thus the entire brain.

Getting down your hands and knees and crawling around like a baby is kind of like reawakening those original connections we made so many years ago. By revisiting them, we make them stronger, reconnect them to a greater degree to every connection that came after that, and so improving the entire system from the ground up.

Stimulating your midbrain in this way feels amazingly good! At first, you might feel incredibly silly down there on the floor, crawling around, looking at the legs of tables and the bottoms of chairs at eye level! But after just a few minutes, you'll feel something amazing happening. The only way to describe it is that you will feel a light, happy, positive emotions — it's seeing the world again as you saw it as a baby. When you were a baby, you had no preconceived notions, no emotional hurts, no hard lessons of life, no cares about money, no worries over personal relationships — you were a clean slate, open to the world and ready to explore with a clear mind and an open and honest heart!

Getting down on your hands and knees is like an instant reconnection with that beautiful child-like state of happy innocence. Better yet, this is not mere speculation, but scientific fact. Think about it. How good would it feel to just be a baby again, if even for an hour on some quite afternoon? Believe us, if you try it, you'll agree it feels great!

Now here's the payoff: if you spend an hour or two crawling around your home on your hands and knees every day for one month, you will be doing a midbrain exercise that will rejuvenate your entire brain and make you feel younger than you ever have before!

Again, the exercise of crawling around on the floor restimulates connections you made with your brain dozens of years ago (depending on your age today!), reinforces them, makes them feel fresh and new, and makes your overall brain function stronger.

Crawling for Brain Power

To get started, find a time of day when you can be alone and undisturbed. No need to create a scene. You don't want to explain to the rest of your family or your roommates why you are crawling around on the floor like someone who has lost a contact lens.

Drop down onto the floor on your hands and knees and just start crawling the way a baby crawls. It will seem odd an uncomfortable at first, but within 10 minutes, your body will began to adjust. You'll very quickly find yourself getting into a comfortable crawling pattern. And guess what? That's not a new skill you are developing. That feeling of increased comfort is the reconnection process. Deep inside your midbrain, the neurons that were formed to develop your crawling skill — neurons which have not been used for dozens of years — are suddenly being asked to contribute again. They like that. They respond by flooded your brain with neurotransmitters — brain chemicals that activate the pleasure centers of your brain.

Pay careful attention to everything. Do just your hands and knees touch the floor, or do you crawl around on your stomach? How is you weight distributed. Are you more on your hands, or more on your knees? Notice the way your knees feel on the floor, the way your hand feel on the floor — and others surfaces — carpet, tile, linoleum, grass (if you go outside) dirt. Can you crawl up steps, or down them? Pay close attention to how it feels. How do you hold your head? Do you stare straight ahead or do you have your head down an survey a small portion of floor at a time? Notice the way everything enters your vision. Do you take everything in or do you find yourself focusing on just what is in front of you?

There is no right or wrong way to do this exercise. Just experience it. The way it will make you feel is the payoff in itself. Don't give up on it after just a few minutes. Let go of the "feeling silly" syndrome. Doing things creatively always feels a little silly and weird, but the benefits are an expansion of your brain capacity. If you do not particularly like the feeling of crawling, that's okay too. You are revisiting and coming to grips with things you may have suppressed or tried to forget in an unhealthy way. To reexperience something like this is to capture it again and file it away right. Wouldn't it be great if you could go back into the past and correct something you did wrong, did not do well, and wish you never did? You can! Crawling like a baby revisits this all important phase in your life which you thought you forgot. It recategorizes it and makes it better.

More Midbrain Stimulation

Now, not all midbrain stimulation exercise is baby stuff. We strongly recommend you do the crawling thing for a month, but also supplement it with other activities that require strong hand-to-eye coordination exercise. One of the first thing that comes to mind is a video game. But if you are anyone over the age of 30, video games are probably just not your thing. There are many adult activities that require close attention to details and sighting details at close range.

Some examples:

- Knitting and other Needle Work
- Painting small intricate works or knick-knacks
- Making a ship-in-a-bottle
- Learning to Type
- Learn watch repair
- Putting together jigsaw puzzles
- Intricate, detailed wood carving

In addition to the above, and you make think of others, you can do exercises, such as jumping jacks, jumping rope, head stands, somersaults, selected yoga exercises, including hand stands, one-leg stands and many others. What all these exercises have in common is that they stimulate the sight-sound-body coordination function of the midbrain.

People who are uncoordinated tend to have poor midbrain development. You've heard it said of someone: "he can't walk and chew gum at the same time." While few people are actually this impaired, such a lack of coordination would point directly to poor midbrain development.

If you have always been an uncoordinated person, doing exercises designed to promote coordination will not only improve your coordination, but a bonus will be better function of your overall brain. Will better coordination make you smarter? It could! That's because your midbrain is so central and connected to so many other important functions.

As just a small example, consider that improving your midbrain function improves your ability to see and hear and process what you see and hear. That means you are processing the information that is coming at you more efficiently. That means you are learning faster! That means you are smarter — and you started it all with some crawling around on the floor like a baby!

The Power of Focus

Another way to improve the midbrain is increasing your power to focus on up-close objects. We touched on this above by recommending a hobby like watch repair. Doing something like watch repair requires you to focus in tightly on small objects, concentrate on them, and put them into a certain order using your higher brain functions.

But you don't have to take up watch repair to improve your power of focus. Instead, try this exercise.

Find a small potted plant. Set it in front of you and move your face in close. Now pretend you are tiny enough to stand next to this plant as if it were a tree. Visualize yourself standing down there next to the trunk of the plant. Now see yourself climbing up the plant, as if you were scaling a large redwood tree. Crawl out on a limb, or in this case, a leaf. Imagine what it is like to be sitting on a leaf, bobbing up and down. Imagine what it would be like to slide down the center of a leaf for a fun flight through the

air and back down to the soft soil of the pot. Imagine yourself leaning your back up against the stem of the plant and
taking a snooze.

How does it feel to be a carefree little elf scaling the
branches of a giant geranium! What does the giant plant
smell like? Can you scale your way to a bright red or yellow
blossom and feel the texture of the soft plant material with
your hands?

Get as deeply into this little fantasy as possible. Then,
when you are ready, end your existence as a tiny plant
pixie, zoom out to become your giant self again. The more
real and the more focused you get into this exercise, the
more mind-expanding the experience will be for you. Once
you have been tiny enough in your mind to scale the stem
of a house plant, expanding out to become your normal self
can be a wild experience. Some people report feeling
"blissed out" by this exercise. Others report intense exhil-
aration. Most report that focusing your mind on a small
object, putting yourself down at that scale, and then
expanding again makes you feel even bigger than you are in
your normal size and life. But this kind of bigness feels light
and expanded, not heavy and giant-like.

Do this exercise as many times as you like, and try many
different variations. Remember that ship-in-a-bottle we suggested you build as a great midbrain exercise? Well, you
could also imagine that you are a tiny sailor on that ship.
You could also picture yourself as the size of a chess piece
and have a fun time hopping across the checkerboard
square.

All this seems like a bunch of crazy kid games, but the fact is, they are powerful exercises for your brain. Again, do them while you are alone if that makes you feel less self conscious. You need to perform these kind of big-to-small visualizations for only 20 minutes a day. The payoff will be brain that is well exercises and improved in function and ability.

Is a brain that is more powerful, smarter and faster worth a few silly, childlike exercises? Absolutely. Many people do other things to harm their brains that are just as silly. Watching idiotic television shows slows the brain down and makes it function less efficiently. Sitting in a bar, getting drunk and acting like a fool is extremely harmful to the brain. As we have said elsewhere in this book, alcohol is perhaps our No. 1 "dumb drug." So why not do some silly exercises to improve your brain function, rather than doing silly things to make things worse?

Okay, enough of the lecture! Let's move on to a discussion of other simply body movements you need to know about if you want better brain function.

The Dual Nature of the Brain

These next exercises take advantage in a breakthrough in the study of brain function that occurred about 20 years ago. The breakthrough was this: every human brain is actually two separate brains. That's right. You have more than one brain in your head. You have two! Astounding as this seems, it is now considered common medical knowledge.

Some would say that there is only one brain, and that one brain is divided into two parts — the Left Hemisphere and the Right Hemisphere. That's probably just as accurate, but semantics aside, the important thing scientists have discovered that Right Hemisphere and Left Hemisphere actually perform different functions.

For example, your left brain is the analytical side. It does all the critical thinking, the logic, the mathematics. The left brain is the pragmatic down-to-earth side of your brain. The left brain is where all your common sense rest, and where the no-nonsense straightforward kind of thinking goes on. The left side of the brain has its feet planted firmly on the ground. It always sees the individual tree as opposed to the forest.

The right side is the dreamer. The rights side of the brain has its head in the clouds. The right side thinks in a nonlinear, symbolic fashion. It's not good with numbers or straight-thinking logic, but is where the intuition resides. The right side is the source of creativity. It's a kind of wild and free thinker that leaps around from fact to fact, not focusing on anything in particular, but always seeing the forrest instead of a single tree.

But as you can see, even though they are total opposites, the left side and the right side need each other very much. They balance each other. Without the right side, the left side of the brain is too rigid. It can only deal in details, while getting creative, and dreaming of "what could be" is beyond it.

On the other hand, the right side does not have its feet planted firmly on the ground. It's full of dreams and grand designs, but does not have the practical, hard-nosed logical thinking to turn dreams and visions into reality.

Nature has developed a way to solve this. It has connected the left brain and the right brain together with something called the Corpus Callosum. The Corpus Callosum is basically a slab of white nerve fibers that connects the two cerebral hemispheres, left and right, and transfers important information from one to the other. In this way, they are able to not only balance each other, but work together. When the right side takes off on a flight of fancy, the left side can take those wild dreams and create something real with them.

The difference between right brain function and left brain function explains a lot about why some people are born to be artists and dreamers, while other are born to become math professors and mechanics. People with an artistic bent tend to be right brain dominant and mechanics tend to be left brain dominant.

Ironically, left brain people tend to be very conservative in their politics, and thus belong to the political "right." Right brain people tend to be politically liberal, and thus belong to the political "left."

A left brain dominant person is more likely to be happy with an organized and/or critical thinking kind of job, anything from working on an assembly line to designing parts for the Space Shuttle as an aeronautical engineer. A right brain dominant person will never last long doing piece meal or repetitive tasks, such as assembly line work, and most often will of make a good engineer. Right brain dominant people are independent, go their own way and are more likely to become painters, sculptors, writers or spiritual leaders. Right brainers tend to be more radical and free thinking, while left brainers tend to be overly concerned with obeying the rules and regulations of society, and are more likely to become dictatorial.

While all of the above is true, brain researchers today agree that the entire concept of right brain and left brain has been overemphasized. If you look around in the real world, you will see very few people who are ALL right brain in characteristic or ALL left brain.

The truth is, most people are a mixture, or a balance of the two. Some people have their head in the stars, but their feet planted firmly on the ground. Some people work on an assembly line all day, but then come home and paint modern art creations. Some people are spiritual, but also intent upon "obeying all the rules," such as the 10 Commandments. Some politicians are heavily liberal, but are also good at organizing their campaigns, and writing the fine details of a complex law.

That's what the Corpus Callosum does. It makes left and right work together to create a balanced, "whole" individual. The greater extent to which this "wholeness" or balance is achieved, the greater the extent to which your brain is functioning at peak efficiency. The reality is, throughout our daily lives we need the talents and abilities of both sides of the brain quite often.

There are many times during the day when we need to think critically, like when we are balancing our check book, and other times when we need more creativity, like when we are decorating our living room.

Opposite Sides

Now here's something that's really weird. While either side of the brain has different functions, the parts of the body they control are opposite. That is, the left side of the brain controls all functions on the right side of the body, while the right side of the brain controls all functions on the left side. Thus, if a person suffers a stroke on the right side of the brain, the left side gets paralyzed, and vice versa. Of course, this immediately suggests that perhaps left handed people tend to be more right brained — thus, left handers are more likely to be, actors, artist and writers. There is some evidence to support this, but which hand you favor doe not tend to be a dominant factor in all this.

Many researchers now believe that doing things to increase the cooperation and balance between you left and right hemispheres is extremely important if we are to improve the functioning of our brains. Fortunately, there are many simple ways, and some high tech ways of getting the job done. We're going to talk about some of the best ones right now.

Cross-Lateral Exercises

These are exercises that take advantage of the knowledge that the left side of the brain controls the right side of the body, and vice versa. By doing exercises that "force" the cooperation between opposite side of the body, you compel the opposite sides of the brain to work together.

Cross opposing
1. Stand up and plant your feet about 18 inches apart. Stretch out your arms to either side, until they are horizon-

tal with the ground. Lift up your right leg, and as you are doing this, bring your left hand down and tap it on your right knee. Do it all in one motion. As soon as your right legs goes back down, lift up your left leg and bring down your right hand to tap your left knee. Then repeat again with the right leg and left hand, and then the other side again. Do this 30 to 50 times.

Many people are surprised how difficult this can be at first, while others find it rather simple. Those who find it difficult may be in more need of left-brain right-brain balance than they thought. Those who find it easy may be more in balance than they thought. The good thing is that a little practice makes this exercise easy. For those with difficulty in this exercise, this provides a golden opportunity to balance the brain and boost brain power.

Note that this exercise does more than improve your coordination. It boosts your ability to think. You can add several points to your IQ. Why? Well, think of your brain as the engine of a car. Some cars have six cylinders, and if just one of them is not working, the whole engine turns sluggish. Your car burns more gas, chugs and grunts and has no pick-up speed. Now, think of our brain. It has only two "cylinders!" The left and the right. If they are not working together, or if one is not working as efficiently as the other, it drags your entire brain function down. Because your brain is "command central" of your body, when it does not run efficiently, nothing does!

Thus, if this simple knee-slapping exercise can improve your brain function by just 5%, you will realize an enormous change for the better in all areas of your life.

Another good example of a cross-lateral exercise is the famous, "rub your belly while you pat your head." Just about all of us have been given this silly challenge in grade school, and for most of us, it was so hard to do it made us laugh! But behind the silliness and the laughter is another key to making your brain function better as a whole. If you still feel silly about it, try this simple exercise again when no one is looking. How difficult is it for you? If it is all but impossible, it may be an indication that the two halves of your brain are not working as closely together as they should be. Practice this exercise until you can do it naturally. Then switch hands. Make sure you can pat your belly and rub your head with equal facility on each side. Once again, you will be doing more than improving your coordination. You will be improving your overall brain function by helping the two sides of your brain to work in greater cooperation and synchronicity

Opposite Hand Writing

One of the hardest things to do is write with the hand that not dominant. That is. if you're right handed, writing with the left is amazingly hard! But there is no reason why you cannot develop your ability to write well and do other things with your opposite hand. The best baseball sluggers are called "switch hitters." That's because they can bat equally well when standing at either the left or right side of home plate, whether or not they are left or right handed. Not all baseball players can master switch hitting. Look at batting averages of some major leaguers and you'll see a big difference in their averages, depending on what side of the base they swing from.

The more you work on your own kind of switch hitting, the more you'll be brining your brain into greater balance. If you are right handed, spend an hour a day practicing writing with your left hand and vice versa if you are left handed. What you will be doing is balancing abilities between your hemispheres. Again, you gain more than a minor skill, such as being able to write well with either hand. This kind of exercise pays dividends across the boards by boosting your total brain function.

Brain Balancing Centers of the Body

People who study the brain and the central nervous system know that there are several places in the body where there are nerve connections that feed directly back to the brain. Some of those areas are on the foot and in the toes. Another is in the lower abdomen. A third is the jawbone. Stimulating these areas with specific exercises in an excellent way to rejuvenate the brain. Let's look at them one at a time.

The Foot

There are specific areas on the foot and within the toes that lead back to the brain. In fact, there is an entire field of alternative form medicine devoted to manipulating these "pressure points" of the foot. It's called Reflexology, and in the past 80 years, it has been developed into a high art.

You might say that reflexology does for through the foot what chiropracty does through the back, neck and spinal cord. By massaging specific areas of the foot and toes, you can send messages directly to the brain, and literally stimulate and supercharge the brain. On the bottom of each of your feet is a kind of map of the entire human body, including the brain.

What's the most important part of the foot as far as the brain is concerned? All reflexologists seem to agree that it is the big toes. The space directly behind the toenail on the backside of each toe is like "Command Central" for the brain. If your brain was a car, this would be the steering wheel and dashboard! From the area behind the big two, you can access directly the major centers of the brain, including the pituitary gland, the pineal gland, the hypothalamus and others. Each of these brain centers are major to your bodily functions and your entire quality of life.

Why is the pituitary so important, and why is stimulating it via the big toe so powerful?

Well, the pituitary gland is also known as the "master gland" in all vertebrate animals, including human beings. The hormones secreted by the pituitary stimulate and control the functioning of almost all the other endocrine glands in the body. Pituitary hormones also promote growth and control the water balance of the body. The pituitary is a small bean-shaped, reddish-gray organ located in the saddle-shaped depression in the floor of the skull and attached to the base of the brain by a stalk. It is located near the hypothalamus.

Thus, stimulating the pituitary gland has a fantastically powerful effect over the entire body

The pineal gland has also been determined to be of absolute vital importance, and the scope of its importance has only begun to be understood. The pineal gland has both neural and endocrine properties. The pineal gland is the body which controls a hormone you may have heard a lot about lately — melatonin. Some call this natural hormone the "miracle hormone" because of all the benefits it can bring to the human body if it is produced in proper amounts. Melatonin, in turn, affects the functions of other endocrine organs such as the thyroid, adrenals, and gonads. The onset of puberty may, in fact, be triggered by changes in melatonin level.

The problem with melatonin in human beings is that, for some reason, the pineal gland produces less and less of it as people grow older. By the time you are 40, you are producing only a fraction of the melatonin you produced when you were a child. And many researchers think that is why old people are "old" and young people are young. The "old" have too little melatonin and the young have it in abundance.

The point for our purposes here is that by stimulating the area behind the big toe with a massage, you can enhance the function of the pineal gland and promote greater melatonin production, which may actually result in a reversal of the aging process! **That's a big payoff for one little toe tickle!**

The hypothalamus lies just below the thalamus on the midline at the base of the brain. It is made up of distinct areas and nuclei. The hypothalamus regulates or is involved directly in the control of many of the body's vital activities and drives that are necessary for survival including eating, drinking, temperature regulation, sleep, emotional behavior, and sexual activity. It also controls visceral functions by means of the autonomic nervous system.

Once again, by massaging the back of the big toe, you stimulate the hypothalamus, and thus improve the way it does all of the above. By stimulating the hypothalamus, you not only improve brain function, you may sleep better, enjoy a better appetite, feel more emotionally balanced and have a greater, or more normal sex drive.

How to Get it Done

So now you know that massaging the big toe takes care of three powerful brain centers, how do you get the job done?

Follow these simple guidelines to produce the best results for toe massage of the brain centers:

Note: You can perform this exercise on yourself, but most experts agree that better results are obtained if someone else performs this massage for you. So ask a friend or a loved one to help you out, or, for best results, you may want to visit a professional reflexologist. Look in your Yellow Pages to find one. This is a rapidly growing profession. A good reflexologist will give you a complete foot workout for about $20 to $25.

1) Remove your shoes and socks. Have your helper use his or her thumb and index finger to grasp your big toe firmly. Use the thumb to rub gently but firmly in circular motions in the area directly behind the toenail. Apply a pinching and squeezing kind of pressure. The massager should press firmly enough to almost hurt — but should stop short of causing actual pain.

2) Continue the massage and move around the perimeter of the toe. Cover the entire area behind the toe-nail with a thorough and vigorous massage.

3) Continue this action for 3 to 5 minutes.

4) After the big toes are done, do the same kind of rolling, firm massage on the rest of the toes, one at a time. Spend 2 to 3 minutes on each toe.

5) Repeat the entire process three times. Total massage time of the toes should be a minimum of 15 minutes, and up to 20 minutes.

If you think this sounds silly, you won't after you give it a try. Have you ever wondered why an ordinary foot rub, say by your wife or husband, boyfriend or girlfriend, feels so extra delicious good? It's because even a simple foot rub stimulates not only the brain, but the pleasure centers of the brain, while it brings into balance vital hormone levels, enhances neurotransmitter flow and synaptic function.

The Diaphragm

Now that we have explored fully the foot and toe exercises for enhanced brain power, let's take a closer look at another important area of brain-body connection — the lower stomach, or as some call it, the diaphragm.

The diaphragm is the lower part of your stomach. For Zen monks and other spiritual disciplines, this part of the body is actually the key to the soul. That's right! You might think the brain, or even the heart would be the most direct doorway to the soul, but a lot of traditional and now scientific evidence points to the lower stomach, or diaphragm, as a powerful source of higher mental thought and experience.

Scientists have recently discovered that in the area of the stomach, including among the digestive tissues and fluids, are many of the same neurotransmitter chemicals that are found in the brain. What are chemicals associated with thought and emotions doing in the stomach!? That's a good question, and medical researchers still do not have an answer for it.

But we don't need to have all the answers to know that stimulating this part of the body can be a powerful way to not only tune up the brain, but to fantastically expand the scope and power of the entire human mind!

What is the best way to stimulate the diaphragm in a way that causes enhancement of brain power? All evidence seems to suggest that the Zen masters have had the answer for centuries — and that answer is: by sitting in the kind of meditation that concentrates awareness on breathing using the diaphragm.

Most of us breath from the top of our lungs. If you will take a moment right now to notice how you are breathing, you are most likely breathing with your chest, and you are taking short, shallow breaths. This is not a very efficient way to breath. For one thing, this is not the best way to deliver oxygen to your brain.

The human brain needs a lot of oxygen to function at peak performance. While the brain comprises only about 2 percent of the body's total mass, it uses a whopping 20 percent of the oxygen taken in. In children, the brain uses even more oxygen. The more oxygen the brain gets, the better it functions. If you could double the amount of oxygen your brain is getting with each breath, think of how much more clear headed you would be. Think of how much easier it would be for your brain to function. Think of how much more alert you would feel. Your memory would be better, you'd feel less tired, energized and all around perkier and better!

The way to double the amount of oxygen your brain gets from each breath is to breath with your stomach and not your chest! This is so important, we are going to repeat it: Learn to breath with your stomach and not your chest. At first, this will seem somewhat difficult and unnatural. But that's only because you are accustomed to breathing the way you probably have been breathing all your life. You may have never realized that there was any other way to breath. But there is. And now we're going to tell you about it.

Pot Belly Breathing

The most efficient way to deliver oxygen to your brain is to breathe with your stomach. You may have to force yourself to breath this way a first, but once you get it down, you will begin to do so automatically.

To get started, sit up straight in a chair, preferably not a soft chair. Use a kitchen table chair or a folding chair so that you have a firm surface under you.

Next, make sure that your spinal cord is straight — that is — do not slump. When you are slumped over, you are not in a position to breath fully and deeply, and as a result, you are depriving your brain of essential oxygen.

Next, just pay attention to the way you are currently breathing. Once again, we bet you are breathing mostly with your chest. Instead of doing this, we want you to take a deep breath by expanding out your stomach. When you breath in, make your stomach push out as if all the air you are sucking in is going down there, rather than into the upper part of your lungs and chest. Hold this belly breath for an count of three, and then exhale the air by sucking in the lower part of your stomach. It may help you to place your hand on the lower part of your stomach at first. Exhale your breath as if you were emptying yourself from the bottom up. Push the air out with your diaphragm. Then, when all the air is out, let the muscles of your stomach expand again, filling your stomach with another bellyful of precious air.

Each time you take in a stomach-full of smoke, hold it for a short three count, and then push the air out with the bottom of your stomach.

This is called "pot belly breathing." Practice it for at least 10 to 15 minutes every day. Again, you may find this difficult to do, and it may seem unnatural. But after just a bit of practice, it will start to feel natural, and before you know it, you will breath this way automatically. The payoff will be enormous. You'll notice that you are less tired and more energetic as you move along through your day. That's because you have learned to increase the steady oxygen supply to your brain. Many people go through life wondering why they are so low in energy, and why they need frequent naps, and why they are prone to depression and negative thinking. Well, shallow breathing may be a huge part of the problem. People that breath shallow from the chest simply aren't feeding their brain enough oxygen. Adopting this new way of breathing is the answer.

Another good way to practice pot belly breathing is to lie flat on your back and place both hands on your stomach. Again, breath in and take the air into your stomach. Feel your hands rise along with your stomach. Hold your breath for a three count, and then push the air out with the bottom part of your stomach. By placing your hands on your stomach, you will have greater control over this process, and you will teach yourself to breath with your stomach more quickly.

Make pot belly breathing your only way of breathing. Your brain will respond in kind with as much as a 75% better functioning rate.

Jawboning

Scientists that study the make-up of the human body know that some 55 percent of all nerves that lead to the brain pass through the jaws. The area of the upper and lower jaw is, then, an important "transfer station," through which more than half of the brain's nerves pass through. Stimulating the jaw with massage, just as you did with the big toes and little toes, will give you a brain-power boost.

Here is how you can best get your jaw massage done.

Sit in a firm but comfortable chair. Sit straight up so that your spinal cord is perfectly straight. Next, place the four fingers on each hand just above the top row of your teeth.

Anchor your hands by placing your thumbs on each side of your chin under your jaw. Then press in firmly with your fingers, massaging the entire area that runs along your teeth line. Work your fingers in a tight circular motion. As you are doing this, move upward and work your way up to your jaw joint, and until you end up in the area just in front of the ears and below the temples. Make sure you massage the underside of your jaws firmly with your thumbs. Give your entire jaw area a stimulating work out. Once again, you will be surprised at how relaxing and rejuvenating this feels. That good feeling is your brain responding to the wonderful stimulation of more than half of its wiring pathway through the jaws.

Working with the Spinal Cord

From the standpoint of the brain, nothing is more important than the spinal cord. That's because the spinal cord is the instrument by which the brain issues its commands to the rest of the moody. The spinal cord is connected directly to the brain via the brain stem. You could almost say that the spinal cord is an extension of the brain itself, and runs down through the body, serving it down to the tip of the toes.

Thus, a supple and well conditioned spinal cord that smoothly transmits the signals of the brain to the rest of the body is vital. What good is a healthy, powerful brain if the signals it sends to the rest of the body don't get through?

So the following, then are a series of exercises that will not only loosen up your spinal cord, and help the brain govern the rest of your body with more efficiency, but will make you feel generally better, more light hearted, happy and healthy.

To get started, first find a place and a time of day where you will not be disturbed for about 20 minutes per session. These exercises can be done anywhere — from your office to your home — just make sure you have some privacy and that you will not be disturbed. Where loose-fitting clothes and prepare a soft, but firm place for yourself on the floor. A blanket or a mat on the carpet should do nicely.

The Snake

1) Lie flat on your stomach, hands by your side, feet together.

2) Place your hands, palms down, beside your waste, fingers pointing forward.

3) Inhale and began lifting yourself up on your hands, bringing the head back and arching the spine as far as it will go. Keep your legs straight. Don't bend your knees — you want to lift yourself up sort of as if you were doing a push-up if your legs were para-lyzed. (You are sort of doing an imitation of a snake).

4) The arms don't need to be completely straight, but keep your pubic area firmly pressed to the floor.

5) Exhale. Bend the knees and now attempt to bring the toes to the back of the head.

6) Hold the pose their for about 15 seconds if you can while you breath in and out normally.

7) Relax and repeat again.

The Corpse

1) Lie flat on your back with your arms at your sides.

2) Slowly stretch out your arms from your sides to above your head and stretch your entire body while taking a slow, deep breath, sucking in your stomach. Keep your mind clear and concentrate on your breathing only.

3) Slowly put your arms back down to your sides as you exhale, and feel your entire body relax.

The Grasshopper

1) Lie on your stomach, hands by your side, palms up.

2) Raise your head and place the front of the chin only on the floor.

3) Make fists of your hands and place them under the thighs in the groin.

4) Inhale, stiffen the body and push down on your arms. Bring the legs up in back as high as they will go.

5) Hold the pose for 15 seconds or as long as you can while holding your breath.

6) Exhale and lower your legs. Relax.

In a previous chapter we outlined the benefits of acupuncture — sticking needles into the body at various points to stimulate the brain.

But we realize that some of you, no matter how painless acupuncture may be, simply cannot stand the idea of having needles poked into your body.

Well, you can still may be able to get the benefits of acupuncture without the needles. The alternative is acupressure — the mere rubbing or massaging of key points on the body, rather than poking needles into those points.

Here then is a 20-minute, 8-step acupressure treatment that will not only boost your brain, but make you feel great all over!

The shoulders :

Use your right hand to firmly squeeze your left shoulder muscle on a point halfway between the base of the neck and the shoulder tip. Do it for 15-20 seconds, and squeeze just hard enough to cause a bit of pleasurable pain, but don't overdo it. Then switch to the right shoulder and do the same thing with your left hand, remembering to concentrate on the midpoint of the shoulder.

Benefits: Relieves fatigue and anxiety.

The temples:

Place your three middle fingers on each temple, close your eyes and press firmly for about 15 seconds. This will relax muscles elsewhere in your body, especially the neck.

Benefits: Can stop pain anywhere in the body because it relieves tension in the neck and elsewhere.

The skull:

Use both hands, press just beneath the base of your skull on the back of your head with your thumbs. Press upward into the base of the outer part of the skull. To obtain the right pressure, tilt your head back. You will feel a dull pain when you are pressing the correct points.

Benefits: Relieves mental tension and headaches. Improves memory and alertness.

The ears:

There are several points on the ear that can be stimulated with acupressure to achieve a variety of results. The fist point is directly behind the ear. Fold your ear forward and place your finger on the mastoid bone, which is just behind your ear. You'll feel it. Working this point relieves a simple earache.

Another ear exercise involves using the thumbs and index fingers of both hands to massage the outer, fleshy part of your ears. Begin at the lower end of the ear lobes and move to the upper part of the ears. Do this twice, taking about 15 seconds each time. This exercise will energize and clear the mind. A third ear point is on the "bridge" of the ear, about a third of the way down from the top and near the front of the ear.

Benefit: Can greatly decrease your brain's dependency on tobacco or some other addicting substance.

The eyes:

Rapid relief for aching eyes can easily be achieved by pressing on a point just in the inside corner of your eye, next to your nose. The left point treats the right eye and vice versa.

Next, rub around the outer rims of both eyes, using medium pressure applied with the middle fingers. Begin at the inner corners of the eyes and move first along the lower part of the orbit toward the temples.

Benefits: The eyes are highly important to brain function. If they don't work well, your brain will not either.

The Hand-Web:

With thumb and index finger, firmly squeeze the fleshiest part of the webbing between the index finger and the thumb of the left hand. Do each hand for 5 - 15 seconds.

Benefits: Powerful headache reliever as well as sinus congestion and arthritis pain.

The Cheeks:

With middle and index fingers, press along the lower part of the cheek bone. Begin next to the nose and move outward to the ears. Take about 15 seconds and do it three times. Benefits: Relieves sinus congestion and tension in the face and head, and improves the complexion.

Benefits: Stimulates the midbrain

To battle depression:

Put pressure on a point on your torso that is halfway between the base of the ribs and the navel. Do it while lying on your back. Also, rubbing the folds of your wrists beneath your hands can lift your spirits from a black mood.

Acupressure is a complex, highly developed ancient practice which reaches far back into the history of the ancient Chinese. In addition to the 8 points described above, there are many other points which have been shown to help everything from sexual disfunction to mental instability.

Conclusions ...

We've covered a lot of territory in this chapter. We urge you to try the many brain exercise techniques we have outlined here — your brain will thank you for it, and you'll thank yourself for giving yourself a more healthy, smoothly running brain and mind.

Chapter 9
How To Amplify Your Brain

If we were to tell you about a simple brain exercise that all of the world's greatest geniuses used ...

... and if we were also to tell you that many scientists believe this simple exercise at least partially caused all these people to become geniuses ...

... would you take up this same brain exercise for yourself?

What if we were to tell you further that this simple exercise could increase your IQ by 20 to 50 points over the next three years, and may even make you a certified genius?

Furthermore, what if this exercise took only 60 minutes a day, and cost next to nothing? No special equipment needed, no special place you must go to — such as a gym or health club — to get the exercise done.

What if we were to tell you that this exercise was extremely enjoyable, and that once you started it, you would experience hours of tremendous pleasure doing it every day?

And even furthermore, what if we were to tell you that this brain exercise is an excellent way to heal emotional problems, overcome grief, and rid yourself of depression, and other mental diseases?

Would you do this exercise?

Would you make it a regular part of your daily routine?

If you knew it could do all of the above, you would be crazy not to, right?!

What is this marvelous exercise?

This: keeping a daily journal in which you write down all of your most important and significant thoughts.

That's it! It's that simple! And it can make you at least 50 percent smarter than you are today.

How do we know that simply keeping a journal can make you a genius? Well, we know for sure that all geniuses — almost without a single exception — kept journals. Albert Einstein, George Bernard Shaw, Sir Isaac Newton, Benjamin Franklin, Ernest Hemingway, J.S. Bach, Leonardo da Vinci, Tom Edison, Henry David Thoreau — all were brilliant and all naturally kept journals from the time they were young enough to write until the time they died.

Researchers have studied journal writing behavior among people and found again and again that the most intelligent, the most artistic, the most powerful and the most successful people of our society almost always keep a journal.

Is this just coincidence? Or maybe it's a preordained aspect of high intelligence to keep a journal, rather than the journal itself that causes high intelligence? The answer seems to be that the journal comes first, the higher intelligence level follows — or at least it gives a greater opportunity for genius to present itself.

Certainly, men like Einstein and Newton were born geniuses, and were destined to do great things — or were they? It is well known that Einstein's teachers considered him slow. Newton also had a great deal of difficulty in his early years of schooling. Yet both of these men changed the very fabric of our existence with their immense contributions to the world's body of knowledge and science. And they were both obsessive journal writers!

Another great genius, Buckminster Fuller, the inventor of the geodesic dome, took journal writing a step further. He kept what he called a "chronograph" of his entire daily existence. His chronograph was not only a journal, but every single thing that came to him every day — letters, notes, memos, and even junk mail and brochures.

The benefit of this, he claimed, was to give him an extremely good idea of who he was in the world. Not only could he see his own thoughts reflected back on himself from his own journal writing, but he could also see what kind of things he attracted into his life, no matter how arcane, or from what source. Fuller reasoned, "If it comes into my life, it must say something about who I am as a person."

In a recent study, several groups of people were examined because they, as a group, seemed not only to live longer than the rest of society, but they also had far less incidence of mental deterioration with age. They had less Alzheimer's Disease, less Parkinson's Disease, less memory loss, and all the rest of the bad stuff that affects the brain.

Some of these groups included Catholic monks from specific orders which required daily journal writing as part of their daily prayer and discipline. Others included a group of housewives who answered a survey as being "persistent daily keepers of diaries or journals."

What the study found was that these people not only lived longer and had fewer mental diseases, they were also smarter than the general population — an average of 30 percent smarter!

Other studies of journal writers all point to the same thing — writing in a daily journal makes you smarter. Writing in a daily journal makes you more resistant to common diseases of the brain, including Alzheimer's.

Why does journal writing do this? Scientists now think they know the answer. The key can be summed up in one word: feedback. When the brain gets a lot of feedback about what it is doing and what it is thinking about, it is somehow able to grow smarter faster, and stay healthier and more solid.

The reason for this appears to be quite logical: more feedback causes the neurons in the brain to grow more thickly. Think of a neuron — a neuron is a brain cell — as a tree branch. Although a neuron is an individual cell, it also contains many branches which extend away from its center, or nucleus. The bottom line is: the more thickly the neuron branches, the better is it able to transmit, store and recall information. That means that thick neurons are smarter neurons. It also means that thicker neurons store not only more memories, but hold more memories better.

This concept has been all but proven in studies with rats. In one particular study, one group of rats was given a very stimulating environment. In simpler terms, they gave the rats a lot of things to do. They gave them swings, doors, ladders, treadmills and other toys. They also ran them through daily challenges, forcing them to use their rat brains and mental power to solve problems that would gain them food.

A second group of rats got nothing. They were kept in dreary blank boxes with white walls and no object to interact with, other than water and feeding tubes.

Still another group — a third group of rats — was put in a different situation. This third group was allowed to watch the rats who had all the stimulating environment with all the toys to play with.

The scientists who were conducting this study reasoned that the rats with the toys would enjoy the greatest brain growth and health because of all the mental stimulation they were provided in their environment.

They predicted the second group would show the least amount of brain development because they had nothing much to do but eat and sleep. They had nothing to activate their minds. Thus, their brains would atrophy.

They predicted that group three — the ones who were allowed to watch the other rats have fun with their toys — to do a little better than group 2, the ones who had nothing. Even though Group 3 did not have their own toys, at least they were allowed to watch and be stimulated by the rats with all the goodies.

The results?

Group 1 — the ones with all the toys and tests — showed spectacular gains in brain mass and brain health In short, these rats were happier, healthier and smarter than the average rat.

Group 2 — the ones with nothing to do or look at — indeed showed very poor brain development, both in terms of brain mass and health, and in their ability to solve problems.

Group 3 — the ones who were at least allowed to watch other rats have fun — did no better than Group 2!

This last result surprised the scientists a great deal. It only seemed logical that Group 3 would be at least a little better off than Group 2. But that was not the case. WATCHING other rats do something interesting was not the same as DOING something interesting. Furthermore, watching was no better than doing nothing at all.

The conclusion from this is obvious. It is not only the stimulation that is important, but also the personal involvement in the stimulation, and the feedback that one gets from that stimulation that truly makes a brain grow more intelligent and more healthy.

The further extremely important conclusion is this: feedback from stimulation is probably more important than genetics, in other words, the smarts and the brains you were born with. Feedback from stimulation is also more important than the kind of outside stimulation you are getting on a daily basis. The fact that you GET FEEDBACK FROM IT whatever is in your environment is more important than what is in the environment.

Scientists now know for a fact that, although all of us are born with a complete brain, 90 percent of the neural development must take place after birth. And the greater the stimulation in the environment, the more thickly these neurons will become. But not we know further than feedback in addition to stimulation greatly increases the mass and the intelligence of the brain.

This is very bad news for people who watch a lot of television. Some may think that watching TV is better than doing nothing. At least a TV program can make you think, and the nightly news keeps you informed. Well, that might be true, but the inescapable conclusion seems to be that watching TV is about the same as sitting in a blank room, staring at the wall and doing nothing. That's because you cannot interact with a TV.

Television programming is a one way street. It feeds you information, and that's it. You need to go further to the next step — take that information and interact with it immediately — to create a healthy exercise for your brain.

The next time you turn on your TV, think of those poor rats who were allowed to watch their buddies, but do nothing else. That's what you are doing when you are watching TV. You are watching a bunch of other human beings doing fun and stimulating things. It's good for them, but does nothing for you. Have you ever wondered why so many TV stars are so rich? Part of the reason is the fact that, to act in and produce TV programming, a lot of stimulating work is required of the actors and producers, just like the rats in Group 1. Actors and producer have the life of Group 1 rats. Those who only watch TV have the life of Group 3 rats.

Actors and producers themselves have very little time to watch TV because they are so busy creating programming for TV. Thus, they get smarter and smarter. Their talent grows and expands. They use that intelligence to get rich, and to produce even more stimulation for millions of viewers.

The same lesson goes for children. It is not enough to provide them with stimulating toys and things to look at. It is a terrible idea to sit them in front of a television set and let them watch colorful moving images for long periods of time. If you want you child to develop into a super intelligent adult with a powerful mind, possibly even a genius, you must give them more than stimulation — you must give them the kind of stimulation that allows them to interact and get feedback.

For example, many people hang a mobile, or toys above a child's crib. This is a good idea because it gives an infant something stimulating to look at. But it would be even better if the child could REACH the pretty objects up there in the air, feel them with his or her hands, bat them about and explore what they feel like. In this way, the child is completing the stimulation-feedback process — the process proven to build brain mass and intelligence.

All this brings us back finally to where we started this chapter — with keeping a notebook or a journal. That's because doing so may be the ultimate way to create the stimulation-feedback cycle on a daily basis in our lives. Just because you have long since left the crib, and even if you are already of advanced age, does not mean that you cannot pick up the stimulation-feedback process now and make it build your brain from the day you start.

There are several ways you can keep a journal so that the process will be effective in building your brain and increasing your intelligence. Let's take a closer look at them right now.

1. Random Writing

Some of the greatest minds in history were fond of writing down any random thought that popped into their head. Perhaps the most extreme example of this is the great Irish writer James Joyce. Most scholars consider Joyce to be the greatest writer of the century, and possibly of all time, with the exception of William Shakespeare. Joyce is famous for his novel, Ulysses, which in large part is "stream of consciousness" writing. In other words, Joyce sat down with pen and paper and wrote down his thoughts as fast as they would come until they started meaning something.

You can do the same. Just carry around a notebook, and whenever a random thought comes to you, write it down. Do not judge it, analyze it or do anything with it except put it down on paper. These thoughts are not good or bad. They are simply thoughts.

But when you right down these seeming random thoughts, you are making yourself more aware of them. Making yourself more aware of your thoughts increases the stimulation-feedback effect which makes both rats and people a lot smarter.

All people who practice this simple technique very rapidly develop greater creativity. We urge you to try this simply brain boosting technique, starting today. Within a week, or even less, you may be coming up with ideas that will tell you how to make more money, how to write a new song, an idea for a new short story or novel, or even a new invention that could revolutionize the world. When you keep a "random thought" journal, you are doing more than stimulating your mind and increasing the power of your brain. You are creating a veritable source book of powerful ideas that may not only change your life, but change the world.

Not only will your notebook become a potential source of life changing ideas, the simply activity of keeping your notebook will automatically make you and your brain more creative. How? By the old psychological standby: classical conditioning. What is classical conditioning? It was first described by the Russian psychologist Ivan Petrovish Pavlov. Pavlov conducted a famous experiment in which he showed a hungry dog a piece of juicy meat. The scent of the meat naturally caused the dog to salivate. At the same time the meat was placed before the dog's nose, Pavlov rang a bell. After doing this a number of times, Pavlov discovered that the dog would salivate just at the ring of the bell, and without having to show it a piece of meat. What had happened? The dog's brain had been trained to associate the ringing bell so closely with the savory smell of meat that the mere sound of the bell triggered many of the same physiological reactions that would have been caused by the presence of true food. The brain had been conditioned to respond in a certain way through repetition and stimulus.

In the same or similar way, every time you write down a perceptive or creative thought in your journal, you reinforce the brain to think creatively and to have new perceptions. What is the ringing bell in this case, or the reward for the brain. Well, most people report that journaling is actually pleasant. It give an immediate feeling of pleasure to write something down. Many times, something unpleasant is written down. This has the effect of "unloading" that unpleasantness, or getting it off your chest. When you get something off you chest, you immediately feel better — the bell rings. Other times, you will be surprised and delighted at how creative you never knew you were before! You write something down, look at it and say: "Wow! I thought of that!" Again, the bell rings.

The more this happens, the more your brain become conditioned to come up with ever more creative and enlightened ideas, until eventually, you are literally a genius! Yes, it can happen to you! All you have to do is keep a daily "thought journal," and before long, you'll have a little book full of miracles.

Now let's look at the opposite side of the coins.

Let's look at what happened when you do not keep a daily journal. Your brain is still thinking perfectly good thoughts, perhaps even brilliant and creative thoughts — but none of them are being captured. For most people, life is one long river of thoughts that flow and pass by every day. Most people never stick a net into that river when something shiny and beautiful passes by. They may even notice a brilliant or creative thought, but then forget about it 10 minutes later when they have to get back to work, or something else distracts them. The brain has no opportunity to get feedback on itself. It has no chance to get a classical conditioning reward. The brain has no chance to hear the bell ring to that it can salivate a new and brilliant idea!

If a dog is never trained with classical conditioning, it will never salivate at the ring of a bell. Why should it? That's preposterous! You can't eat a bell made of metal and wood! Similarly, a brain that is never rewarded for the brilliant ideas it is constantly producing will never learn to recognize those ideas clearly, and will never take action upon them. Furthermore, a brain that does not get rewarded for each of it's brilliant ideas will have little incentive to produce more of them.

So ring the bell for your brain. Write down all your good ideas, and your bad. The good ideas will condition your brain to come up with even more. The bad ideas will be unloaded from your soul, and won't be a further drag on your life.

Since we mentioned it, let's talk a little more about the negative things that may be floating around in your mind.

and the fact that many people get caught up in these negative things and end up reinforcing them again and again.

We all know people who are cranky all the time. We all know people who are perpetual "negative thinkers." Perhaps your mother or father was a negative thinker, or a pessimist. If they were, they very likely passed this mental condition, or habit, on to you. Negative thinking is like a germ disease — it's extremely contagious.

Children of negative thinkers are especially likely to grow up to be negative thinkers themselves, and in turn, pass the trait onto their own children. And the cycle goes on. That's why some families stay poor for generation after generation, and why other families maintain wealthy dynasties that go on for generation after generation. An example of the latter might be the Kennedy's or Rockerfellers.

Negative thinking is the result of the very same thing we told you that could make your brain into a positive, creative, idea generating machine: good old classical conditioning — or in this case, bad old classical conditioning.

No child is born negative. Each new baby has a fresh new brain just waiting to be conditioned by its environment, and more strongly, the people in the environment. If the child is surrounded by negative thinkers 24 hours a day, guess what? That child is going to become a negative thinker too! Even when a baby is newly born and only a week or two old, what the adults are saying and talking about in the presence of that child are being registered and stored away for future reference.

Imagine a new-born baby riding home from the hospital in her new parents' car, and mom and dad are having a conversation that goes something like this:

Dad: "Well, now we have another mouth to feed. I don't know where I'm going to find the money to raise this kid up right the way it deserves to be!"

Mom: "Look, I know we're poor, but we've always managed to get by somehow before. We'll make it. We'll cut back on this and that, and we'll raise this child good enough — if not rich, at least with food on the table and clothes on its back."

Dad: "Yes, I suppose you're right ... but I can't help worrying about what's going on down at the plant. There's a lot of talk about cutbacks, and I'm first in line to be laid off. And you know how far an unemployment check goes, not to talk about losing our health insurance coverage."

Mom: "Well, don't expect me to pitch in any time soon. I've been carrying this load in my stomach for the past nine months! I'm exhausted! I need a vacation, not a second job!"

Dad: "Well, if the new baby begins to starve I'll bet you'll have to find a new job soon enough — we just have to make ends meet."

Mom: "How am I going to find a job? I have no skills, no college eduction. The only thing I can get is a minimum wage job, and that doesn't pay enough to take care of day care! The more I work, the more we'll get behind!"

Dad: "Well, I sure as heck can't get two jobs! The one I have now is killing me the way it is! I wish we would have been more careful. The last thing we need right now is another mouth to feed."

Mom: "You're right. We've got a tough road ahead of us, so we might as well get used to it."

And the baby is listening to every word! This kid hardly has a chance!

True, the baby may not be understanding all of this yet, but studies prove that even a newborn infant is absorbing the conversation and language around him or her, and is very likely storing it away for future reference. Indeed, some scientists believe the things a newborn baby hears in it's first weeks lay the pattern for the entire personality of the person he or she will eventually grow up to be.

But negative feedback is not only with many of us from birth. We also encounter it every day, in school, at work, from relatives, even from television and the other media. Perhaps we should say, especially from television. Studies show that each child is exposed to some 20,000 acts of violence — from killings to rapes — on TV every year. Again, remember Pavlov's dog. Ring the bell, smell the meat, ring the bell, smell the meat. Most of the time, when a child is watching TV, they are also receiving mild rewards. Often they are eating tasty snacks, or enjoying the company of friends. Sometimes they are just rested and relaxed. And while all of these rewards are set in place, the child is being shown violence, lewd sexual behavior, news reports of muggings, bombings and war, and the list goes on.

Think of all the other negative stimulants that were forced upon you throughout your life. How many of you had a teacher that you would never amount to anything? How many of you had a bosses who mistreated you on the job and used scare tactics and threats to keep you in line and coming to work on time? How many of you were told you would "go to hell" from some minor transgression by a clergyman of church official. All of us have, at one time or another.

And we want to mentions one more jaded and cynical stimulus before we move on to the solutions to overcoming this kind of conditioning.

Perhaps one of the primary negative stimulation in our society is the pressure to conform. Say what you will, but the human animal is a group animal, and most people are followers. The pressure to conform and to go along with the group is not only enormous and ever present, but almost irresistible for the average person. Our society is one that frowns on "being different" for the most part. Although some people are lifted up and praised for being different — such as certain artists, musicians and scientists who have "made it" — the average person on the street or in your neighborhood faces intense daily pressure to conform to the "norms" of society.

But what just about everyone forgets is that, before the stars of our world "make it" and becomes heroes for doing something great with their creativity, they were most likely ostracized, frowned upon, and very likely, laughed at and mocked cruelly for being who they were, or for daring to do something different.

The difference between a person who is considered a societal outcast or a fool is usually money and fame. If your foolish and contrasocial behavior gets you rich and makes you popular, then you are not seen as a fool, but as a genius, artist, or creative spirit.

Yes, our society is extremely two-faced when it comes to members of the crowd who dare to be different. Ninety-five percent of the time, a person who is different is a fool. The other 5 percent are the elite of our world who were able to "rise above the herd" and become someone or something special.

In two interesting study done by psychologist at the two different major universities, the strength of the pressure to conform was made very evident.

In the first study, one test subject was placed in a room of 20 or 30 people, and all of these people except the test subject were "in on the experiment." The clued in people were given these instruction. At the front of the room on a big screen, certain objects would be presented, including lines, squares, circles and other shapes,

For example, two lines of obvious different lengths were put up on the screen. The group was then asked to raise their hands when the instructor pointed to the longer line, and keep their hands down when he pointed to the shorter lines.

But all of the clued in people were instructed to raise their hands and vote for the wrong line — even when one line was obviously longer than the other.

The idea was to see if the test subject would choose the correct line, even if it meant going against the group opinion.

Well, you can just about guess what happened. In most cases, the test subject ignored reality and went along with the group, even in the face of a difference so obvious, that even a chimp could have picked the longer line from the shorter line.

Again and again, the test subject was swayed by the opinion of the group, and even in the face of hard physical reality, did not dare buck the trend and stick with the truth.

The second test shows something equally interesting, but something more sinister.

In this second test, a test subject was asked to give quiz to another test subject, who was hidden from him behind a wall. The tester could not see the testee, but they were allowed to hear the person on the other side so that they could ask them questions as receive answers.

Also, and this is the interesting part, the tester was told that the test taker on the other side of the wall was hooked up to a number of electrodes throughout their body. The tester was also given a button which he was to press to give the other person a shock whenever they got an answer wrong. Furthermore, the tester was also given a dial that could increase the severity of the shock on a scale from 1 to 10, where 1 was a mild shock and 10 was extreme pain.

But now here is the catch: the person on the other side of the wall was not really hooked up to anything. They would get no shock, and had no electrodes taped to them. Rather, they were instructed to only act like they were in pain when the tester gave them a shock — that is, make verbal sounds of pain that the tester could hear through the intercom. They were further instructed to cry out louder in agony when the tester cracked up the pain meter to giver higher and higher levels of punishment.

So the shock receiver was in on the test and was only acting, and the shock giver was being tested to see how far they could be pushed to go in administering punishment to a fellow human being.

The idea was to test how willingly people will obey orders, especially when that order is given to them by an authority figure, in this case, the psychologists who were running the test.

The result? Just about every test subject went right ahead and administered what they believed to be maximum pain to the fellow human being on the other side of the wall! Although some of the test subjects objected to giving painful electric shocks to other people, they all eventually obeyed, especially when goaded on. The actors on the other side all could have won Oscars for their performances. They cried out in blood curdling agony as the questioner cranked the pain intensity button from "mild shock" to "brutal electrocution." Nevertheless, the shocks were given. All people followed instructions and justified it by the using the same phrase so many Nazi war criminals used: "I was only following orders."

What can we conclude from this interesting, although troubling experiment? This: the average person is very much bent on conformity in our society, including nearly blind obedience to authority figures. Even when confronted with a situation that strongly violated their personal ethics, sense of fairness and humanity, they jettisoned all of the above for the sake of "going along."

What else can we learn from these two studies? Well, these studies and others like them should be a wake up call to any of us who have become too complacent with our current mode of existence.

These studies also show how deeply ingrained the conditioning is of the average American citizen. Many of you reading this probably are saying to yourself: "If I was the test subject of either of those two studies, I would have identified the correct line," or "I would not have given my fellow human being a shock!"

But are you sure? Because you are reading about these studies from the stand point of an outside objective observer, it is easy to point the finger at where others have failed, but if you were an unsuspecting person participating in a study like the ones above, are you sure you would be any different from any other human being?

What we should take from this is a desire to become more independent in our thinking. What we should take from this information is the courage to understand that to be different is not necessarily bad, and very often, is good. Always following the crowd, and never having the courage to stand up for what you think is right and just limits your ability to become a creative thinker, an innovator, and a person who stands out from the rest. Just about all of us like to think that we are "special."

But when the chips are down and in difficult situation, how different are we, really? Each day, are you doing what you can to make sure you are not laughed at or criticized by "the pack." Are you the kind of person who does not like to make waves? If you are, you may be playing it safe, but you also may be crippling your own ability to be creative. You are holding back your own brain. You have caged up your spirit in favor of a "safe haven" where nothing new or exciting can ever happen.

Starting today, take a closer look at your life and ask yourself honestly:

"Am I a follower or an innovator?"

"Do I go along with the crowd, or do I forge ahead, leading the way?"

"Before I make a decision, do I stop to see what every one else has done first, and then just go with the majority, or do I examine my unique role and position in the universe, and then take bold action based on my own intelligence and intuition?"

"Am I afraid to make mistakes?"

"I always like to play it safe, rather than take responsibility for my own thinking."

Yes, playing it safe keeps you out of a lot of trouble, but playing it TOO safe holds you back and makes you just another anonymous sheep in the flock. So don't laugh to hard at the guy or woman in your neighborhood who always seems to be "going his own way." Different does not always mean bad. Different very often means creative. You should dare to be different more often. Your brain will grow more powerful as a result.

What about Negative Feedback

We don't want to leave this chapter until we give you some tools to deal with and defeat negative feedback.

No doubt, no matter how well you were raised, you received negative feedback at many times in your life. Remember the example of the parents with the new baby, and their pathetic conversation filled with an overwhelming load of pessimism and negative thinking?

Well, fortunately, there is a powerful new way to "deprogram" even this heavily ingrained kind of negative programming that may be lodged within your mind right now, blocking your brain from achieving more, and blocking you from realizing your highest potential as a human being. Furthermore, this new method cannot only clean up your old "negative tapes," but can also install new "positive tapes" that will make achieving even greater things easier than it ever has before.

What is this powerful new technique. Well, most people call it simply "NLP." NLP stands for Neuro-linguistic programming. It's easy to do, requires no special equipment or professional services, and it can easily change your life.

In the next chapter, we'll tell you all about NLP, and how to use it.

Chapter 10
The Key To The Programming Of The Brain For Success

In the centuries of the human search for ways to bring out the greatest hidden potential in all of us, only in the past 10 years has one of the best methods ever been developed to get the job done. It's called NLP.

Just what is NLP? Before we tell you what it is, we want to tell it what it can do for you.

- NLP can transform a depressed person into a happy person.

- NLP can change a fearful person into a confident person.

- NLP can change bad memories and into sources of strength and hope.

- NLP can change your negative programming into positive programming.

- NLP can change negativity into deep wisdom

- NLP can change channel anger into the energy to make things better.

- NLP can turn an unmotivated, lazy person into a super achiever

- NLP can turn nightmares into dreams come true.

- NLP can change with a poverty mind into a prosperity mind.

- NLP can transform a lost soul into a well balanced human being at piece with the world and with a positive place in the world.

And the list could well go on.

But we think that's enough. So just what is NLP? Well, NLP stands for *Neuro Linguistic Programming*. Now that you know what it stands for, you probably don't know much more! But don't be afraid of these fancy words. We'll explain and de-mystify them right now.

Neuro refers to nerves, or in this case, the nerves that serve your brain, bringing it information, and sending information back from brain to the rest of the body. Neuro in this case also refers to neurons, which are what individual brain cells are called, as you have read elsewhere in this book.

Linguistic refers to language. That's because a lot of the information that is stored in our brains is done so in the format,rules,etc.

form of ordinary human language. We should be clear that we are talking about that information which includes higher thoughts in this case. Obviously, most of the information stored in the brain is not language, or verbally based. For example, the brain knows how to keep your heart beating, but that information for that purpose is not stored in actual language within the brain that commands every second or so: "Make heart beat ... make heart beat ... make heart beat ..." No, the heart beats involuntarily and is handled by that part of the brain which stores involuntary information for running all the biological systems of the body.

But much of the stuff that makes us truly human are those thoughts that make us objectively aware of ourselves as independent beings existing within a greater universe or environment that is our home.

These kind of thoughts are stored verbally, or by language. For example, when you think: "That's a lovely sunset!" that is a specific thought, and the chain of words which make up that thought are actually encoded within the neurons of your brain. The method of that encoding is chemical. Most people think of thoughts as "invisible," and not exactly "real," although most people really don't think about the nature of thoughts at all.

But the fact is, thoughts can be said to be real physical "objects." That's because each thought is made up of a specific combination of brain chemicals. The brain's chemical units, or thoughts, use the neurons of the brain like a highway to travel around on. When you are thinking thoughts, you are actually activating these chemical units. As you "think thoughts" you are moving all kinds of specially encoded chemicals around in your brain.

These chemicals are very powerful, and truly miraculous. For example, remember that beautiful sunset you saw at the beach that one summer? It was so spectacular it took your breath away, and you still remember it vividly to this day. Well, that memory is really nothing more than a specific group of chemicals stored and encoded within your brain. Whenever you want to recall that beautiful sunset, the brain activates the chemicals that represent that image of a sunset and then "run them" through that part of the brain that causes you to see a mental image of the scene.

Not only are good and beautiful images stored in the brain via verbally encoded brain chemicals. All the bad stuff is handled the same way. Remember the time the teacher bawled you out and humiliated you in front of the class for not having your homework done? That's a mental code stored on your brain. When you remember this incident, the brain activates those chemical units which make up this memory and run them through your brain, causing you to revisit this painful incident in your mind.

In a sense, you might say that these images are "programmed" into your brain using verbal units made up of brain chemicals. So we see that the term NLP, which stands for neuro linguistic programming, refers to the way all our good thoughts and our bad thoughts exist within the structure of the brain.

And by this point you may be asking: "So what? How can this knowledge help me change my life for the better? How can knowing how thoughts are stored on the brain change my personal sadness into happiness, or my weaknesses into strengths?

The answer can be found in the process of the way your brain programs and stores information. You see, the fact that all of your thoughts are stored in your brain verbally means that, in a very real sense, you have direct access to them, just as you would have direct access to a your tax files which you keep stored in a desk drawer.

At any time, you can go to that desk drawer, open it, take out your tax files, and change the information that is recorded on them if you really wanted to. (Of course, you could change them in such a way that would get you into trouble with the IRS!) That means you don't have total freedom to do whatever you want with the information. That's not the point. The real point is that if you wanted to, you could change the numbers on your tax forms to any numbers you wanted them to be whether they were the proper numbers or not.

In the very same way, you can have access to the files - the memory files – that are stored on your brain and alter them in any way you want. Because your memories are stored verbally, you can actually go into your brain and re-write those words to make them something more to your liking.

Let's present several examples of what we mean by this.

Many people have been programmed to be negative thinkers by their parents. Without knowing that they are doing so, many people teach their kids to have a sour outlook on the world, and they teach them to believe that "everything goes wrong for them" while all the "other" people get all the breaks.

Poor people often tell their children: "Sure we're poor, but that doesn't mean we're bad people. Look at all those rich movie stars. They go through five or six marriages each, get hooked on drugs and many of them even commit suicide. Look at Judy Garland. She killed herself. And Mick Jagger is a rich rock star but he's been a dope addict most of his life and he can't seem to remain faithful to his wife. And look at Donald trump. He's twice divorced and everybody hates him. You don't want to be like that, do you?"

Here we see a prime example of early programming that is probably keep the child who hears it poor for the rest of his life. After all, he doesn't want to end up killing himself or getting hooked on drugs like those rich successful people. This child has been neuro-linguistically programmed into equating being rich and successful with miserable failure.

What the child does not know is that the examples given above are the exception and not the rule. Most people who are rich are happier than people who are poor. But you never hear much about rich happy people. Why not? Because it's not very interesting. When millionaire heiress Patty Hurst was kidnapped and later found to be cooperating with her captors as they robbed banks, the media went wild for this story of a "little rich girl gone bad." Why would a millionaire rob a bank?

Such sensational facts make for good news. But a rich girl who stays home, gets a college eduction and later becomes a successful banker is absolutely boring. Why would any newspaper write a dry and uninteresting story like that?

The public wants scandal, and they get it. There's always a handful of rich and famous people screwing up and making a mess of their lives. We all know Liz Taylor has been divorced eight times and that billionaire Howard Hughs was a freaky recluse who was deathly afraid of germs. But what we don't hear as much about are the thousands of rich people who live quiet happy lives full of freedom, adventure and prosperity.

Studies prove that rich people live longer than poor people. Studies prove that rich people are happier than poor people. Studies prove that rich people even tend to be more spiritually attuned that poor people. They also get divorced less, not more than poor people, and they are far more likely to help out their neighbors than are poor people.

But the myth of the "noble poor" is a persistent one in our society, and even middle class people tend to warn their children against greed and losing one's soul to money and materialism.

Anyway the point is, by telling a young person that to be poor is be noble and proud, and to be rich is to be shallow and empty, you are programming that person to think and act in a way that will keep money away from them probably for the rest of their lives.

The brain chemicals of that person become deeply set within the neural pathways of the brain. Again and again, the words: "poor is good, rich is bad" circulate through the brain and like a well-programmed machine, the person acts out this command in his or her daily life. They don't even try to go to college because it costs too much money, and money can't make you happy anyway. They don't save money because if you get too much of it, you might become one of those crazy rich people. You don't go for the good, high-paying jobs because those are only given to people rich enough to have college degrees. You don't try to start your own money-making business because everyone knows it takes money to make money, and having money is dangerous. Wasn't it the Beatles that said: "Money can't by me love."

Because this is so important, let's take an even closer look at how millions of people get negatively neuro linguistically programmed right from the first day of their infant lives.

Imagine a new-born baby riding home from the hospital in her parents' car, and mom and dad are having a conversation that goes something like this:

Dad: "Well, now we have another mouth to feed. I don't know where I'm going to find the money to raise this kid up right the way it deserves to be!"

Mom: "Look, I know we're poor, but we've always managed to get by somehow before. We'll make it. We'll cut back on this and that, and we'll raise this child good enough — if not rich, at least with food on the table and clothes on its back."

Dad: "Yes, I suppose you're right ... but I can't help worrying about what's going on down at the plant. There's a lot of talk about cutbacks, and I'm first in line to be laid off. And you know how far an unemployment check goes, not to talk about losing our health insurance coverage."

Mom: "Well, don't expect me to pitch in any time soon. I've been carrying this load in my stomach for the past nine months! I'm exhausted! I need a vacation, not a second job!"

Dad: "Well, if the new baby begins to starve I'll bet you'll have to find a new job soon enough — we just have to make ends meet."

Mom: "How am I going to find a job? I have no skills, no college eduction. The only thing I can get is a minimum wage job, and that doesn't pay enough to take care of day care! The more I work, the more we'll get behind!"

Dad: "Well, I sure as heck can't get two jobs! The one I have now is killing me the way it is! I wish we would have been more careful. The last thing we need right now is another mouth to feed."

Mom: "You're right. We've got a tough road ahead of us, so we might as well get used to it."

AND THE BABY IS LISTENING TO EVERY WORD! THIS KID HARDLY HAS A CHANCE!

True, the baby may not be understanding all of this yet, but studies prove that even a newborn infant is absorbing the conversation and language around him or her, and is very likely storing it away for future reference. Indeed, some scientists believe the things a newborn baby hears in it's first weeks lay the pattern for the entire personality of the person he or she will eventually grow up to be.

But negative feedback is not only with many of us from birth. We also encounter it every day, in school, at work, from relatives, even from television and the other media. Perhaps we should say, especially from television. Studies show that each child is exposed to some 20,000 acts of violence — from killings to rapes — on TV every year. Remember Pavlov's famous dog? Ring the bell, smell the meat, ring the bell, smell the meat.

Most of the time, when a child is watching TV, they are also receiving mild rewards. Often they are eating tasty snacks, or enjoying the company of friends. Sometimes they are just rested and relaxed. And while all of these rewards are set in place, the child is being shown violence, lewd sexual behavior, news reports of muggings, bombings and war, and the list goes on

Think of all the other negative stimulants that were forced upon you throughout your life.

- How many of you had a teacher that told you would never amount to anything?

- How many of you had a boss who mistreated you on the job and used scare tactics and threats to keep you in line and coming to work on time?

- How many of you were told you would "go to hell" from some minor transgression by a clergyman of church official.

All of us have, at one time or another.

It all adds up the a brain programmed — neurolinguistically programmed — to be negative, to think in perpetual terms of scarcity, of being poor, of being afraid and all the rest.

This attitude permeates every aspect of your life, including your business life. Even if you have been trained and educated in how to be a successful business person, that training is resting on a foundation of negativity and fear-based hardwiring in the brain. So while you go through all the right motions of doing business and making money, it's a struggle the entire way. Something always seems to go wrong. Opportunities always seem to be missed. The competition always seems so much better than you. Other in the office have an advantage over you. Sure, you make a living, but every dollar you earn feels like a pound of flesh being ripped off your body.

The reason is deeply embedded and programmed negativity which is so deep that you don't even know that it has a daily control over you.

Here's what amazing: Even though the majority of people are operating under the grinding oppression of a brain that is hard-wired to be fearful, negative and limited, they still go on to achieve positive things in their lives! Most people pull themselves up to a middle class lifestyle which, if not filled with luxuries and magical adventures, is at least not a total hell. You have a roof over your head, a car or two, lots of material possessions, from VCRs to CD players, fulfilling relationships.

What this says for the strength of the human soul is enormous. Most people accomplish positive things every day while the weight of the world programmed into their brains.

Of course, millions of other people succumb to the baggage that is hung on their souls from the time they are babies. The millions of poor people, the homeless, the addicts, the criminals, the human parasites of society (both rich and poor!) are the victims of brains that have been programmed to bring them to the lowly point where they exist in misery every day. So while the majority of people achieve middle class status, a large percentage do not fair as well.

And somehow, a small percentage of people come into the world and receive programming that is mostly positive and uplifting. They don't necessarily have to be born rich. Most often they are not. They are born with something even better — parents who hard-wire them from birth to be positive and proactive in their most fundamental thinking processes. These are the sparkling people we read about in newspapers and magazines, and see on television. These are the great people of history — the top 1 or 2 percent of human society — who go where everyone else cannot, who make the world a better place than it was before, who float above the masses like super men and women. (Note: As you'll learn later in this book, a small percentage of these "super people" actually achieve stunning things for just the opposite of positive wiring! Negative wiring can drive human beings to great lengths. You'll learn all about it in an upcoming chapter)!

Here is why the new science of NLP is so exciting and holds so much potential for the human race: because it can transform any person with negative wiring into one of those elite people with positive wiring! Better yet, NLP is not something that requires you to see a psychologist at $90 an hour for 10 year; it does not require that you attend a $500-a-day seminar with some high-profile motivational speaker and author; it does not require any fancy or expensive equipment to work for you; it does not require hours or year of disciplined study or meditating, or anything else.

NLP is free, and yours to use in any way that your unlimited and creative mind can find ways to apply its power. NLP is a tool that can reverse your entire lifetime of negative programming. NLP can not only reverse negative programming, but replace it with the opposite — positive, joy-filled programming that can lift you up from your daily struggles with your existence to the kind of life that seems to defy gravity itself!

NLP does this by getting at the most basic and fundamental aspect of your existence — the very chemicals that make up the thoughts which add up to make — YOU! When you change your thoughts, your change reality.

Remember, we said that you can access any thought in your brain and change it as easily as you would the information on your tax forms. With a little practice, you can turn a painful memory into something that is positive.

Remember this: NLP is something that takes place entirely in the mind. You might say that it does nothing to manipulate the outside world of solid reality, but don't be so hasty in that judgement. We would remind you of what the great Swiss psychologist Carl Jung once said: "Consciousness precedes being." At first, this may seem like a cryptic, mystical comment, but when you give it a bit of thought it's actually a very powerful statement about real life.

Jung was hinting at the fact that without human consciousness to perceive the world, in effect, there would be no world! This is kind of like that old mind bender: "If a tree falls in the woods and no one is around to hear it, will it make a sound?"

The answer is no. It will only make the POTENTIAL for sound. Because, after all, what is sound? Sound starts out as shock waves traveling through the air. When these wave hit the outer ear, they are grabbed, aimed and sent into the inner workings of the ear, including all those little bones, tubes and inner ear fluids. All these tiny bones and structures transform the shock waves into nerve impulses. Those nerve impulses travel to the brain and are sent along the billions of neural pathways that make up the corridors of the human brain. Once in the brain, the nerve impulses made from shock waves are "manufactured" or interpreted into what we human beings called sound.

In light of this complex process, can you still think of the shock waves created by a fallen tree to true and complete sound? No, the tree only created the raw materials for sound. Sound become sound only after a human being makes it complete.

What is true for sound it also true for all of the other senses, from sight and smell to touch and taste. When you frame the tree question using some of the other senses, it almost sound absurd.

For example, one might ask this: "If someone cooks a steak and no one eats it, does it taste good?" Or: "If the sun sends its rays through a cloud of airborne water particles will a rainbow be created?"

Can a steak taste good all by itself — without being eaten! Does a rainbow exist without a human being to complete the circle by seeing it?" Again and again, the answer is no. All of these things out in the environment are only the first half of what we call reality. The second half of reality is manufactured inside nature's most awesome miracle — the human brain!! The brain is literally the projector of reality. It harvests raw materials from the physical universe and shapes them into the kind of things that human beings surround themselves with to call reality.

So without human beings all we have is a universe of potential, or a Potential Universe, if you will. What this also means is that, at every moment, at every instant, we human being are creating our own reality in a very literal sense. What this also means is that a chronically negative person is going to be creating a chronically negative reality. That's because all the raw materials coming into him from the Potential Universe are being created by a brain that is biased toward negativity. A positive person creates an insistently positive and happy universe. That's because all the raw materials of the Potential Universe are being filtered through a brain that is bent on seeing the good aspect of everything.

From this point of view, we can see how a person "literally" creates his or her own reality.

If you think this is amazing, wait, there's more! The argument we have been making about human beings literally creating their own reality has more of a basis than what we have been talking about so far. Without getting too much into all the hairy details, we must mention that the science of modern physics, specifically quantum physics and quantum mechanics, also strongly support the idea that human beings are in a constant process of literally creating the universe with their consciousness. These conclusions come out of the work primarily of Werner Heisenberg, Erwin Shrodinger, Albert Einstein, Arthur Eddington, David Bohm and several more.

These men have put forward the theory of the Universe as a vast container of potential energy and information which is ready to be formulated and shaped by the kind of devices that can convert all this potential energy information into a recognizable kind of reality. The human brain is such a device. Again, to go into the mind-boggling realm of quantum physics here would be beyond the scope and intent of this book. We mention it, however, to give you the confidence that the NLP tools, techniques and strategies we are about to give you not only work, but that they are based on a foundation of scientific fact that has been put forward by the greatest and most brilliant minds of all time.

NLP puts your hands on the keys of creation itself. You already have a reality creating miracle machine, your brain. In this book we are going to show you how to use your creation machine more efficiently and in a way that brings you absolutely anything you want in life.

Please note that the reality creating quality of your brain works on more than just rainbows and sound from falling trees. It works on EVERYTHING. That means you can create the kind of reality you want in every aspect of your life. If you want the perfect marriage, NLP can help you have it. If you want to get rich in business, NLP can make it happen for you. If you want to have a closer relationship with God, NLP is a gateway to even that spiritual realm.

While the primary focus of this book is going to be using NLP to improve your sales, business and financial life, we are doing so under the proposition that a prosperous business life does not occur in a vacuum. To many people conquer the world of business only to loose their marriage, their family or their souls in the process.

Moving Things Around With NLP

Imagine that you are sitting in a theater watching an extremely exciting movie. It's one of those movies with such a good plot, believable character and eye-popping special effects that you are drawn into the experience, even forgetting the moments at a time that you are sitting in a theater hall with bad seats and a sticky floor. During those moments when you are totally absorbed, that IS your reality.

Even so, somewhere deep in your mind there is an aspect of you — Your Eternal "I" — that never quite goes to sleep the whole way. It will draw you back to your normal reality when it sees fit. It doesn't mind letting a greater part of your Self enjoy a fantasy for a while. Sometimes, a vacation from "normal" reality is just what's needed.

But we all know the feeling of "losing ourselves" in a good movie or in the pages of a good book. While you are involved in the movie or book, you are what is called "associated" with it. Writers and artists call this phenomena "the willing suspension of disbelief." That's because you are your suspending your knowledge that you know that what you are watching is only a movie. But in order to have more fun, you "willingly" suspend your disbelief. Willingness is a key word because it makes the case that you have a choice about what you want to believe and what you don't want to believe, and when.

At other times, you can be the opposite — dissociated from the object or situation of focus. If the movie is bad, it's difficult to get into it. You are much more aware of your own thoughts of disgust for the bad art you are viewing. You squirm in your seat a lot more and you are more aware that your left shoe has a large wad of gum pressed to the bottom of it. In this case, you do not suspend your disbelief, willing or otherwise. If a movie is a load of crap, why give up your normal reality to be absorbed in a pile of crap?

Either way, whether you are in the driver's seat. At your will, you can choose to be associated with an experience or disassociated from it. This is extremely important and is a central key to everything you will be learning in this book.

There are many times and situations in your life when it will be advantageous for you to be highly associated, excited and involved with a situation, and other times when it will be much better to be cool and dissociated from a situation. Many times our emotions and close involvement with something can destroy our objectivity and best judgement about that situation. Other times our lack of interest means that we don't have the motivation we need to pull us through something that needs to be done. In this case, more association with the situation would be of greater advantage.

Think about this: What if you could get yourself more closely associated and involved in all the wonderful and positive feelings and memories in your mind and what if you could turn down the volume and minimize all of your bad memories and experiences so that they stop dragging you down. No, we're not talking about a dangerous denial kind of behavior in which you do not learn valuable lessons from past mistakes, but rather, the ability to make a past hurt STOP hurting once the lesson is learned.

Let's face it: being hurt again and again by something has a diminishing point of returns, to borrow an axiom from the field of economics. At some point, you earn the right to eject a thorn from your soul, a thorn that is nailing you down and preventing you from from going on to achieve greater things.

Imagine taking an inventory of every hurt, humiliation, painful experience, rejection and disgrace in your life and being able to watch them from your inner being, leaving you feeling free, light and as forgiven as an angel after receiving grace from the Highest Sources! NLP can help you clean out the dross from your life that is holding you down. At the same time, it can help you turn up the sensory volume on all the good, positive and pleasant moments of your life so that your will rest not on a bed of nails but on a cushion of confidence, happiness and self assurance. A peron functioning in the later vain is more prepared to excel at whatever he or she chooses, be it business, sports, personal relationships, or social situations.

Let's give all this theory a test run right now. Let's run through a little exercise that will give you a real example of how this works.

NLP works best when done from an extremely relaxed state of mind and body. If you are the kind of person who has no idea about how to get yourself in a deeply relaxed condition, we suggest that you investigate the many excellent methods for doing so. You can find dozens of books and tapes on inducing relaxation within yourself. We are not going to go into it in great detail here, but we want to make it very clear that the deeper your state of mental and physical relaxation, the more powerful these NLP exercises are going to be for you.

So first, start with the relaxation technique of your choice. Make sure you take three deep breaths, paying close attention to how the air goes in and out of your lungs. Next, clear your mind of cluttered thoughts. Most people's minds race with jumbled thoughts of all kinds — practitioners of Zen call this "Monkey Mind." Do the best you can to "clear the airwaves," so to speak. Also keep in mind that you will never totally clear your mind. To not think is something that is alien to human experience, although Zen Masters claim that years of meditation can bring about this experience, or non-experience. When that happens, they say, you will achieve a higher state of consciousness, but this is a whole other story.

For our purposes, and what we can learn from experienced master mind calmers is this: it's best not to force your mind into a state of quiet. Rather, a more passive approach generally works the best. Don't so much attempt to stop your thoughts as detach from them. Think of all of your thoughts are a rushing river. Most of the time we are caught up in that river and are carried along. What you should try to do is step out onto the river bank where you can see the water flow by while you stay still. Don't try to stop your thoughts, just watch them go buy. Once you free yourself in this way, you'll find yourself in a much calmer, deeper, more magnificent state of being. It takes practice, but anyone can do it.

But now let's get back to NLP. After you achieve a greater or lesser degree of relaxation, think of an experience in your life that was extremely pleasant. Pick something that brings up no-holds-barred good feelings for you. Once you have it, notice how you feel. Then make these feelings grow even bigger. There is no right way or wrong way to do this. Using your mind, increase the pleasantness of the the memories by getting closer to them, and perhaps by blocking out anything else. Get totally into the experience as if your memory was a movie screen and you could magically walk up and get inside the movie. Notice how you feel.

Now, start shrinking the whole scene out and away from you. In your mind, distance yourself from the pleasant memory, until it seems that you are looking at a small, square TV screen of the event from across a large room. Notice again how you feel about the event. Notice that when you are further away from your pleasant scene that your emotions are less activated, smaller and less attached.

Most likely most people reading this never realized before that they could actually get inside their mind this way and start playing around with things! Don't worry — it's not dangerous! Rather, just the opposite is true. What you are doing is taking your first steps to getting control over your own mind and your own life.

After all, you won your own mind. You can do what you want with it!

And this is a tremendous power. We've only just begun, but we've already shown you a way to bring happier, more positive emotions closer to yourself, changing the way you feel. If you can make something good come closer to you, you can also do the opposite — make something bad go further away.

Try it. Pick out something painful that happened to you in your life. Again, and even if this hurts at first, put yourself in the scene and notice the level of pain it brings you. Notice your feelings carefully. You may even want to quantify or rate your level of pain on a scale of one to 10. Now that you have your evaluation of your pain level, move the scene away from you in whatever creative way that you want. Picture your painful moment as a picture in a frame, and then make that framed scene move away from you, shrinking down to the size of a stamp. Once the scene has gone small, look at your pain scale. For most of you, the pain grew less, even if by a little. Remember that one of the keys to this exercise it NOT TO GET CAUGHT UP in your bad or positive thoughts. Bad thoughts especially have a way of grabbing us and forcing us into a circular wheel of bad feelings, recriminations, regrets, wishes and fantasies about revenge, and so forth. Don't let this happen. DETACH! Enlist the power of your imagination to play a kind of game with all this. Think of yourself as a magical movie director who, at will, stop action on your mental scene, pull in closer, move away, or do whatever is desired.

Once again, most people are amazed to learn that certain painful events which have tormented them for years can suddenly be "turned down" or even "turned off" completely! And even if you achieved only a slight effect, we assure you that as you practice the conscious manipulation of your own memories and feelings, you'll get better and bette at it.

Perhaps you have something that is not a memory but is bothering you right now. You have an ongoing problem. Maybe a situation at the office, or a neighbor is making your life miserable. Well, you can't shoot your neighbor and get rid of him (well, you can but you'll go to you'll fry in the chair!) but you can distance yourself from the noxious feelings this situation is generating. Why would you want to do that. Isn't this a form of denial? No, it's just the opposite. You see, many times in life we can't see obvious solutions that are right before our eyes because we are too wrapped up emotionally in the situation.

By framing the situation in your mind and then putting mental distance between yourself an it, you are not denying problem, but actually taking a better look at it. You are looking at the problem from a new, clear-headed perspective. Once you have a new perspective, all kinds of solutions you could not see before may present themselves, and soon your problem could be solved. At the very least, you could prevent this ongoing problem from taking a daily toll on your life. If you can't get rid of the problem right away, at least you can turn down the volume on it so it doesn't ruin your life!

So we have just given you some powerful NLP visualization tools which, in and of themselves, can change your life!

Conclusion
This is only the Beginning....

In this book, you have learned about foods, vitamins, herbs, hormones, drugs, exercises and special techniques to make your brain more powerful and more healthy than it is today.

More than any other time in history, human beings today have at their fingertips the tools to go beyond the ordinary abilities of an unaided brain.

It's up to you to pick up these tools and put them to use. You can't take advantage of brain boosters of all sorts if you don't take action to bring these wonders into your life.

While you avail yourself of the current tools and technology to boost your brain power, remember this – this is only the beginning! The science of brain and mental enhancement is just getting started. Indeed, as you read this, scientists all over the world are working hard in their labs, developing new and exciting substances that may soon make geniuses of us all!

Most futurists predict that within 10 to 20 years a whole battery of safe and powerful drugs will routinely be taken by just about all people, drugs that will boost our IQs by dozens of points, and drugs that will easily blow away depression, or brain diseases, such as Alzheimer's or Senile Dementia.

The future looks bright. The ability to tap into the brain's full potential is at our doorsteps. We have much to look forward to. The powerful brains of human beings are relentlessly shaping the the destiny of all of us, taking us even beyond the realm of mind and biological substance, to a future none of us can yet imagine, but which all of us will certainly share.

Index
Unleash the Power!

J

Journal writing, 220, 225

K

kelp, 72

L

Lecithin, 158
Licorice, 68
Life Extension, 153

M

Ma Hung, 65
Marijuana, 137
massage, 204, 209, 213
Meditation, 111
Memorization, 46, 47, 49, 172
Microalgae, 81
Minerals & Gemstones, 69
minerals, 79
motivation, 22, 237, 239, 251
Mushrooms, 71

N

negativity, 25, 26, 223, 230, 238, 245
Neuro Linguistic Programming, 240, 255
neurotransmitters, 75, 86
Norepinephrine, 74
Nutmeg; 68
Nutrition, 11, 58, 70, 91, 145, 156

O

Oats, 70
Old Age Brain, 52
Oxygen, 88, 92, 141, 205
Oxywater, 89
Oyster shell, 71

P

Parkinson disease, 154
peppermint, 72
Phenylalanine, 86, 92
pituitary gland, 202
Protein, 59

R

Ruby, 69

S

Sage, 68
Sarsaparilla root, 73
Seeds, 72
Selenium, 80
serotonin, 14, 75, 136, 180
Silicon foods, 72
skullcap, 73
sleep, 99, 148
Smart Drugs, 92, 135, 138, 140, 147, 166
Sprout Juice, 80
St. John's Wort, 181
strength, 29, 38, 53
Studying, 36

T

TV, 223

V

Vitamin A, 85, 91, 156
Vitamin C, 81, 91, 156
Vitamin D, 16, 91
Vitamin E, 79, 84, 91, 156
Vitamins, 79

W

wheat grass, 80
wood betony, 73

Y

Yin Yang, 71, 124

Z

Zinc, 80

OTHER HEALTH AND MONEY BOOKS

The following books are offered to our preferred customers at a special price & postage paid.

BOOK	PRICE
1. Insider Guide To Government Benefits	$26.95
2. CREDIT SECRETS	$26.95
3. Guide for Free Cash Benefits For 50+	$29.95
4. Proven Health Tips Encyclopedia	$17.95
5. Foods That Heal	$19.95
6. Healing & Prevention Secrets	$26.95
7. Most Valuable Book Ever Published	$14.95
8. Book of Home Remedies	$28.95
9. Book of Blood Pressure & Cholesterol	$28.95
10. Penny Stock Guide & newsletter	$49.00
11. Learn to Trade Options & Make Money	$149.00
12. Guide to Prostate Problems & Treatments	$23.95

Please send this entire page or write down the names of the books on another sheet of paper and mail it along with your payment .

NAME OF BOOK_____PRICE_____
NAME OF BOOK_____PRICE_____
NAME OF BOOK_____PRICE_____
NAME OF BOOK_____PRICE_____

TOTAL ENCLOSED$_____

SHIP TO:
Name_____
Address_____
City_____ST_____Zip_____

MAIL TO: AMERICAN PUBLISHING CORPORATION
          BOOK DISTRIBUTION CENTER
          POST OFFICE BOX 15196,
          MONTCLAIR, CA 91763-5196